GREAT CAESAR

GREAT CAESAR

PLANTAGENET
SOMERSET FRY

COLLINS
St James's Place, London

William Collins Sons & Co Ltd
London · Glasgow · Sydney · Auckland
Toronto · Johannesburg

First published 1974
© Plantagenet Somerset Fry 1974
ISBN 0 00 195372 9
Made and Printed in Great Britain by
William Collins Sons & Co Ltd Glasgow

CONTENTS

FOREWORD

All children have their heroes of history. My favourite was always Julius Caesar, ever since the time a Latin master introduced me to Caesar's Gallic War. I remember so well being told: this is the military autobiography of the greatest man of action in the history of the world. At first I could not see what was so remarkable about this Roman who kept leading 'our men' against one almost unpronounceable tribe after another, who 'threw' a bridge across the Rhine. But I was greatly impressed by the portrait busts of Caesar photographed in the school text book, and I longed to find out more about him. As luck would have it, very soon afterwards, Shakespeare's Julius Caesar was given to us as a set book, and in the hands of a sympathetic English master with a strong sense of the excitement of history, the whole drama was unfolded.

We were steered towards further reading, and I fell upon books about Caesar by John Buchan, Warde Fowler and J. A. Froude. I was very moved by the build-up to the assassination, and by the deed itself. It was not difficult to imagine how lost and empty the Roman people must have felt when they heard about his death. People felt much the same when President Kennedy was assassinated in November 1963.

As I thought about Mark Antony's reaction to seeing his friend's bloodstained corpse, put so well by Shakespeare, 'Thou art the ruins of the noblest man that ever lived in the tide of times,' I took it to mean the greatest man and could see why he said it. Of course Caesar was not perfect. Of course there were some regrettable incidents in his career. But over the last thirty years I have not found any reason to change my view.

What is a 'great man'? The Concise Oxford Dictionary has it; 'a man of remarkable ability, genius, intellectual or practical qualities'. This would fit many famous men of action in history, some of whom, indeed, came to be known as 'the Great'.[1] But

---

[1] Alfred, king of England, Alexander of Macedon, Canute of Denmark & England, Casimir of Poland, Charles, king of the Franks (Charlemagne), Akbar of India, Frederick of Prussia, Peter of Russia.

it fits Caesar better than anyone else. Whatever attitude to Caesar historians (especially modern ones) take, they find themselves compelled in the end to admit that in him was combined an unparalleled accumulation of talents. This seems to me to support the contention that Caesar was the supreme man of action in world history. The story of his life which follows will, I hope, justify this contention.

ABBREVIATIONS OF NAMES

A.	Aulus	P.	Publius
C.	Caius	Q.	Quintus
Cn.	Cnaeus	Ser.	Servius
D.	Decimus	Sex.	Sextus
L.	Lucius	T.	Titus
M.	Marcus	Ti.	Tiberius

to John Hunter

I loved and admired him, so how could I
approve of his murder?

CAIUS MATIUS 44 BC

Thou art the ruins of the noblest man
That ever lived in the tide of times.

MARK ANTONY in Shakespeare's
Julius Caesar C. 1600 AD

The entire and perfect man.

THEODOR MOMMSEN 1856

Yes, he is at the top.

WINSTON CHURCHILL 1959

But it still remains impossible to think of anyone
who has ever united a more spectacular
and varied collection of talents.

MICHAEL GRANT 1969

I

MASTER OF THE ROMAN WORLD

There had been a thunderstorm in Rome during the night of 14th March, in 44 BC[1]. The rain had been exceptionally heavy and the level of the great, rolling river Tiber had risen sharply, threatening to go over the top of its banks down in the poor district of the Suburra. When the sun came up the next morning, the huge paved streets of the city began to steam as the water was dried off. Chinks of sunlight flashed through the gaps between the tightly-packed buildings in the Forum and seemed to bounce off the richly polished pink and white marble columns of the new Julian market hall which was nearing completion. Everything looked clean, as if in preparation for some great display or presentation.

Just below the Palatine Hill, one of the seven hills on which the ancient city was built, which towers over the Forum, stood a large white house. Outside the main front porch were several guards, helmeted, with short swords in their scabbards. There was a lot for them to do, checking entry passes, examin-

[1] The vernal, or spring, equinox falls on about 20th March, a time of unsettled weather.

ing leather wallets and satchels, directing a stream of visitors
to different rooms and offices, callers who began arriving
almost as soon as it was daylight. For this was not only the
home of Julius Caesar, dictator, and the most important man
in the Roman Empire. It was also his suite of offices, and all
manner of people constantly called on him or his staff for
favours, help, commissions, authorities, of one kind and
another.

On the first floor, in a small dressing room, Caesar was
getting ready for another full day's official and administrative
business. Today he was going down to the Senate to receive
their blessing for his approaching expedition against the
Parthians, hundreds of miles away in Syria. There would be
offices of state to fill to preserve order and to supervize his
new institutions while he was away. There would be authorities to grant and sign for a host of undertakings. And there
would be the usual run of petitions to read and consider.

Caesar put on his toga and adjusted its folds carefully, as
was his invariable habit, for he always paid special attention
to his dress. Then he girded his waist with a belt which he
wore loosely. A servant, meanwhile, tied up the leather
thongs of his sandals, and another handed him his wreath of
laurel leaves. He liked wearing this, not only because it had
been an honour voted to him by the Senate and people of
Rome, but more so because it covered up his balding head,
about which he was strangely self-conscious.

Then he picked up a sheaf of papers and a stylus and walked
swiftly out of the room, down the wide marble staircase and
out through the porch where he was saluted by the guards.
He returned their greetings with some friendly words, and set
off down the Via Sacra into the Forum and then along the
street which led to the Theatre of Pompey. The hall adjoining
this was being used as a temporary Senate House, as the old

building had been burned down some years earlier during a serious riot.

As he walked along, several citizens looked up at him, for he was very popular among the ordinary people of Rome. This tall man, with well proportioned limbs, still slim in spite of his fifty five years, had dark, flashing eyes, a pale complexion, and a straight high nose. By now there were wrinkles about his firm but kindly jaw and furrows across his broad forehead, betraying a certain tiredness, but he had not lost the good looks which had been remarked upon widely in his youth and which had dazzled many women throughout his adult life. But there was something else singling him out as apart from other men. By 44 BC his countrymen had begun to regard him as semi-divine, while in the provinces he was already being worshipped as a god. In Rome, men felt secure when they saw him or heard him speak. He had become their protector and they in turn had sworn not to let him come to any harm.

As Caesar approached the hall, a man rushed up to him and thrust into his hands a document, urging him to read it at once. It contained full details of a plot against his life, involving nearly sixty senators, most of whom owed him everything, money, position, lands, some even who had plotted against him before and had been spared. But if the man said so, Caesar could not have heard, for he put the document among the other papers in his left hand and carried on into the hall. There he saw an unusually large gathering of senators, chattering away. When they espied him coming through the doors they quickly divided into two rows to make a path for him up to the special chair which the Senate had decreed he should be allowed to occupy whenever he attended their meetings. It was of gold and was more of a throne than a chair.

Caesar sat down as the senators took their places, and called order for the meeting to begin. Suddenly, some of the senators rose from their seats and moved slowly towards Caesar, menacingly. One was Tillius Cimber, whose brother had been banished by the dictator some time earlier. He begged Caesar to end the exile. Cimber's pleas were supported by the other senators who now gathered round Caesar's chair. They included Marcus Brutus, Caius Cassius and Decimus Brutus, three men among many who had received special favours from Caesar. But Caesar had no intention of retracting the sentence – it had been richly deserved. When he refused, Cimber fell on his knees and clutched at Caesar's toga, pulling it down. This was the signal for the men round Caesar to draw daggers from the folds of their clothes. Caius Casca lifted his arm and brought it down on to Caesar's neck. 'This is violence!', cried Caesar, as he grabbed the arm and ran his stylus into it. But at once the senators closed in on him, stabbing and slashing, most of them wildly, some even cutting each other in their frenzy.

After a while they withdrew, still holding their blood-stained weapons, and as they did so, they saw the object of their murderous attack stagger around blindly. Several daggers thrusts had cut open his head and his eyes were filled with blood. Then the wounded dictator, realizing he was going to die, drew the top of his toga over his head and let fall the bottom part to cover up his feet, so that he would die with dignity. He sank to the ground, close to the statue of Pompey, a man who had once been his son-in-law and friend and then, reluctantly, his enemy. For a moment his body shuddered, and then, as the life went out of it, lay still, the left hand still clutching unopened the document which could have saved his life.

It was the 15th March, the Ides of March in the Roman calendar. Some weeks earlier a prophet had warned Caesar to beware of the Ides of March, but he had carelessly ignored him. Thus died Caius Julius Caesar, Dictator, Father of His Country, whose life the entire Senate had sworn to protect against violence.

There was an irony about his assassination. By removing the man who was changing the face of the Roman World the conspirators succeeded in making it certain that those changes would come and that they would be permanent. The effects of his achievement reached immensely far and are with us still, as one recent historian[1] has said. This is easier to understand when one remembers that no one in history combined excellence in so many fields of human endeavour. Caesar was was at one and the same time a general, a statesman, a lawgiver, an orator, an historian and a mathematician. As a general he never lost a war; as a statesman he left a system of government which, with modifications, lasted for centuries. As a lawgiver, he transformed municipal government. As an historian he wrote one of the best accounts of a war of conquest[2] of all time, a success for which he himself had been responsible. As a mathematician he re-structured the calendar, whose benefits we still enjoy today. His career, as it unfolds in the remaining chapters of this book, amply testifies to what must seem an exaggerated combination of talents.

Attitudes to Caesar's career have varied considerably over the centuries. Those of a liberal mind have deplored his autocratic rule and his contempt for the republic which he made little effort to disguise in his last years. The humanitarians condemn the excesses of slaughter and sometimes cruelty which were features of some of his campaigning in Gaul, and they believe that his famous clemency in the civil wars was

[1] Michael Grant: *Julius Caesar.*
[2] De Bello Gallico: his commentaries on the Gallic War.

motivated less by a sincere abhorrence of violence or a bigness
of heart than by sheer needs of policy. In our age, in which
the very idea of dictatorship is unacceptable, whatever good
it might do for a country, Caesar is sometimes thought of as
being one of the worst kinds of tyrant, such as Hitler. The fact
remains, however, that whatever people have thought they
have acknowledged, even if in some cases grudgingly, that his
career stands unique in the story of the world.

Cicero, a contemporary of Caesar and a lover of the old
republic, congratulated the conspirators for murdering Caesar
but had to admit all the same that he was the greatest man he
had known. Suetonius Tranquillus, the second century AD
historian, no admirer of the Caesars, wrote a book about the
first twelve, in which Julius received more favourable criticism
than all the others. Plutarch, a Greek biographer who was at
heart a republican, said that Caesar's achievements bore away
the palm.

When the scholars of the Renaissance in Europe unearthed
the remnants of Latin and Greek literature and history, they
were thrilled to find support for their long held belief that
Caesar had been the greatest man of the ancient world. They
saw Charlemagne's conception of the Holy Roman Empire
in western Europe (the great political ideal of western
Christendom) as a logical extension of Caesar's imperial
dream. Although they recognized – as all Christians did – the
existence of only one God, they found it perfectly compatible
to accept the semi-divine nature of Caesar and perhaps would,
if he had been a Christian, have made him the patron saint of
Europe. Dante, the great Florentine poet, who was also a
widely read and profound thinker, portrayed (in his Divine
Comedy) the Devil in Hell, with three men beside him. One
was Judas Iscariot, who betrayed Jesus Christ; the other two
were Brutus and Cassius, Caesar's principal murderers. That

Possibly Julius Caesar as a young boy

Renaissance men concerned themselves with Caesar's career and achievements is amply demonstrated in their art. Pictures illustrating some aspect or other of his life abound.

The greatest playwright in the English language, Shakespeare, picked on the drama of Caesar's murder and the character of his assassins to construct one of his best tragedies. To bring into focus the differing motives and emotions of Brutus, Cassius, and Casca and others he had to play down the real Caesar, or else the conspirators would be dwarfed. But here and there he let through what was still the prevailing view of Caesar. Mark Antony calls him 'the noblest man that ever lived in the tide of times'. The appearance of Caesar's ghost shows how Caesar was destined to be a mightier force after death than before it.

In the nineteenth century, when people thought about and worked harder for political liberty than ever before, Caesar was still regarded as the greatest man of the ancient world. Professor Mommsen called him 'the entire and perfect man'. J. A. Froude described him as a man whose aim was from first to last better government. If the Mommsen comment was an overstatement, the Froude assessment was what many historians to-day would accept.

Then at the start of the present century, when some scholars had perhaps become irritated by the paeans of Mommsen and his followers, Sir Charles Oman called Caesar a brilliant opportunist, dealing sanely and practically in turn with each problem that came before him, but a splendid criminal who made an end of laws and liberty, a man in love with power. But he also admitted that Caesar did more perhaps than any other single man that has ever lived to shape the future destinies of the world.

After the First World War, when many of the shattered nations of the world began to reconstruct themselves under the guidance of elected or self-appointed dictators, Caesar once more came into his own. G. M. Trevelyan, the historian, wrote that Caesar showed how the outworn machinery of the ancient world could be reconstructed on new principles. Sir Winston Churchill, one of the very few world figures in the same class as Caesar, by virtue of his many-sided genius, once said to his physician, Lord Moran, that 'Napoleon was a very wonderful man, but I put him after Julius Caesar. Yes, he is at the top.' John Buchan, the novelist and classical scholar, said Caesar performed the greatest constructive task ever achieved by human hands, and laid the foundations of a fabric of law and government which is still standing after two thousand years.

Perhaps the supreme achievement of Caesar was that in his last years he restored the confidence of the Roman people in themselves. His reforming work was so well advanced that once his great nephew, Augustus, had reached the same position of eminence fifteen years later, he was able, with little difficulty, to continue the work, which resulted in a

This portrait bust of Caesar is in the British Museum. For many years it was
believed to be the best likeness of him, and it was used in every book about him
or his times. In recent years, however, it has been argued that it is not authentic,
but is an 18th century likeness sculpted in Italy from earlier busts.

period of peace, order, reconstruction and prosperity in Rome and the provinces that lasted, with very few intervals, for two hundred years.

What was the secret of Caesar's success? It was a combination of two things: the unique versatility of his talents and an unequalled capacity for imposing his will upon other people. A large part of his life is the story of his getting people to do what he wanted them to, not only in the advancement of his own career but more especially in the great reconstructive work he saw he must do if Roman civilization was to survive. How necessary this work was and how he achieved it is what this book is about.

II

BEFORE CAESAR

At the time of Caesar's death the Roman world had reached its greatest extent since Rome was founded seven hundred years before. It stretched from the Belgian coast to the Black Sea, from Portugal to Palestine. Its landmass, covering well over a million square miles, almost completely encircled the Mediterranean, making the Mediterranean a Roman sea. The only comparable civilization in the world at the time was China, far away in the East, and while both empires knew about each other, and even traded, no official contact had been made. Neither was any danger to the other. Rome was undisputed mistress of her sector of the globe.

It had not been like that for long. Seven hundred years earlier, Rome was a tiny settlement on the banks of the river Tiber in Italy. Peopled by members of the Latin race which lived in the central part of the peninsula, it had been founded by one of their chiefs, Romulus, in 753 BC, who became Rome's first king. For nearly two and a half centuries the city was ruled by kings, but in the last years of the sixth century, the seventh king, Tarquinius Superbus (Tarquin the Proud) governed so badly that the people rose up against him and

Gaius Marius, Caesar's uncle and seven times consul.

drove him out. He had started off by murdering his predecessor, Servius Tullius, and usurping his throne. Then and there, in 509 BC, the Romans decided never to have a king again. In his place they elected two consuls, who were to govern jointly for one year only, when two more would be elected for the next year, and so on. The first two consuls were Lucius Junius Brutus, who had led the revolt, and Caius Collatinus. Other officials were appointed on a yearly electoral basis later on. This was the beginning of the Roman system of republican government.

Tarquin's rule must have been exceptionally severe, for the very idea of kingship was to be abhorrent to all Romans for centuries to come. Indeed, one of the reasons advanced by conspirators who murdered Caesar was that they believed he

Lucius Cornelius Sulla, dictator from 82 BC *to 79* BC.

wanted to become king of Rome. And one of the slogans most frequently shouted by the conspirators when they lifted up their bloody daggers over the dead dictator was 'Long Live the Republic!'

It should not be thought that Rome made no progress under the kings. Most of them were good rulers, particularly Servius Tullius, who surrounded Rome with a great wall. When the republic was created Rome was already a large city, its buildings and streets sprawling over seven hills.[1] It had a complex and efficient drainage system, the Cloaca Maxima, it had several fine palaces and temples, and it had the Circus Maximus, a huge oval-shaped race course for chariot

[1]The Capitoline, the Aventine, the Quirinal, the Esquiline, the Caelian, the Palatine, and the Viminal.

racing and athletic contests. These athletic contests were an important feature in the lives of the Romans who were, in the earlier centuries, a tough, stern, disciplined people who believed in keeping fit so that they could work very hard at their farms and industries when they were not at war and fight with great courage and endurance when they were.

It was in the time of Servius Tullius that the differences between the classes of society came to be defined. The upper class, the patricians, were the privileged ones. They were free men, they had money and land, and many belonged to a body called the Senate which advised the kings. They were for the most part descendants of the first people Romulus brought to Rome. The lower class, the plebeians, were freed slaves or strangers visiting Rome who had decided to stay. There was a wide gap between the two, and it was to grow wider over the years. It was not helped, when the new republic was created, by the rule that only patricians could be candidates for high office. The plebeians were allowed to vote at the assembly of the people it is true, but this privilege was not worth much if none of their own number could hold high office. It was nearly 250 years before the plebeians really had full legislative powers in Rome, and when they did, it did not serve to bring the two classes any closer together.

The history of Rome from the beginning of the republic to the middle of the third century BC is really the story of how, externally, the Romans strove to make themselves masters of Italy, and how, internally, the plebeians struggled against the patricians for a say in the government. By 265 BC the Romans had defeated all their enemies in Italy,[1] and had welded them into a league of Italian nations of which Rome was head. By that time, also, plebeians could stand for the consulship.

---

[1] Up to a line between the river Arno on the west and the river Rubicon on the east.

A print by Veronese, in 1681, of the Circus Maximus as he imagined it was in Roman times. The site and some foundations have survived.

Once they were masters of Italy, the Romans began to look beyond it. And when they did they came up against the empire of Carthage, a state of Phoenician origin in North Africa, with colonies all along the North African coast and the eastern coast of Spain, in Sardinia and the western half of Sicily. This great power was the chief trading nation in the Mediterranean, a position it kept by means of a huge fleet of ships and an almost inexhaustible supply of troops from its subject territories.

The Romans had had little experience of naval warfare, but once they saw what sea power could do, they directed their energies to the long term aim of wresting from Carthage its dominion over the Mediterranean. In 264 the first Carthaginian or Punic War broke out when the people of the city state of Messina, in the east of Sicily, appealed to Rome for help against Carthage. The Romans responded, and at once set about building a fleet of ships, and teaching themselves how to handle them in conditions of combat. The war lasted for about twenty three years. Although Carthage was defeated in several engagements and lost both Sardinia and Sicily, it was no decisive triumph for Rome. There remained in Carthage a war party determined to crush the growing power of Rome in the Mediterranean.

Twenty years later, the young Carthaginian general, Hannibal, one of the greatest military commanders in all history, invaded Italy from Spain, making his famous crossing of the Alps on the way. In an astonishing campaign he beat every army that the Romans sent against him, and at Cannae in 216 he inflicted well nigh the most devastating defeat ever dealt upon a Roman army. A Roman force of perhaps some 85,000 was cut to pieces, over 50,000 were slain in the field. There were hardly any troops left to defend the city, if Hannibal wished to march upon it. The Roman commander-

The amphitheatre at Nimes in France

in-chief, M. Terentius Varro, limped all the way back to Rome, but instead of being arrested for his failure, he was greeted by a delegation from the Senate thanking him for not despairing of the republic.[1]

At this moment, Hannibal's own government in Carthage took it into their heads not to send him the reinforcements he needed for the siege, because they were jealous of his successes and feared his power. The golden chance to break the power of Rome slipped away. Instead, Hannibal ravaged large areas of Italy until he heard that the Romans were sending an army across the sea to North Africa to attack Carthage itself, where-

[1] The Senate also freed and armed the slaves in Rome and prohibited public mourning for the dead. A Carthaginian general in a similar situation would almost certainly have been crucified.

upon he returned to take command of the defence. At Zama, in 202, he was decisively beaten by Publius Cornelius Scipio,[1] and the second Carthaginian War was over. All Carthage's overseas territories passed into Roman hands. Fifty-six years later, without any provocation, the Romans invaded Carthage, now a small community in North Africa, and after a two-year siege overwhelmed its capital city, Carthage. The buildings were razed to the ground and ploughs were drawn across the site, removing it, as it were, from the map forever.[2]

A few years after the destruction of Carthaginian power, the Romans also overcame king Philip of Macedonia who had dominated the Greek city states for some time, and in doing so they gave the Greeks their freedom. Then they defeated the attempt of king Antiochus of Syria, who had tried to re-create the empire of Philip in Greece.

Rome was now mistress of the Mediterranean. As a result of her conquests, great riches began to flow into the city, riches that even the wealthiest Roman had only dreamed of but never seen. Gold, jewellery, new building materials, foods, clothing (especially silks), corn, iron, all manner of things arrived in great quantities in an almost unending stream of transport ships. And along with these luxuries came hordes of men of many nationalities, captured in war on land or at sea, and women and children taken from the cities and fields of Greece, Carthage, Syria, Macedonia, Spain, creating a vast pool of human slaves to do the work in the houses and streets of Rome and in the countryside of Italy which had hitherto been done so diligently by the Romans and their allies. These people had for centuries been farmers working out their lives on small holdings. When the country went to war, they had

[1] Scipio received the title Africanus for his victory.

[2] Carthage was rebuilt as a Roman colony by Caesar after the battle of Thapsus in 46 BC.

dropped their spades and put away their ploughs, taken up their arms and armour and headed for the nearest military assembly point. Even their leaders sometimes came straight from the fields. When the city was threatened by the Aequi, in 458, the Senate sent for the foremost soldier of Rome, Lucius Quinctius Cincinnatus, and offered him the command of the army. Cincinnatus was ploughing his fields at the time and at first refused, saying he had to get the work done before dark. The delegates beseeched him, and he gave way. He trudged off to his small cottage, took off his working clothes, donned his toga and lifted a sword and some armour off the wall. Then he set off for Rome where he was appointed dictator for the duration of the struggle.

They stayed on to see the war through, unless they were injured, or killed. Then they returned home and took up their farming again. If the war was successful for Rome, they usually ended up with rich rewards of booty of one kind or another. But now, in these altered times, when they returned, they were likely to find that greedy land speculators had bought up their farms. So they drifted into the cities, especially to Rome, there to eke out their service bonus as best they could.

All this proved too much for the austere, simple, hard-working Romans, and their very character began to change.

It is one thing to win a series of wars and so acquire an empire. It is quite another thing to govern it properly. From the time of the Punic Wars, the Roman government became increasingly inefficient. They cannot be blamed, for they had no real experience. They were, moreover, wedded to the idea of electing or appointing officials for a period of one year only (with few exceptions), and while this may not always have been a handicap in the city, it could not work well in the provinces. Governors did not have enough time to get to know their provinces, the people, the languages and customs, or the religions. The temptation to make money from the heavy taxation imposed by Rome, and from selling favours was impossible to resist, and since they were as a rule only in post for twelve months, there was a fair chance of making a fortune without getting found out before the year was up. As their successors in office were usually as easily tempted, they could be relied upon to cover up any unpleasantness.

This pursuit of wealth was by no means confined to provincial governors or officials. It became a way of life in Rome itself. The simple and hard-working Roman changed into a grasping, pleasure-seeking spendthrift who was quite happy to lead an idle and aimless life while the new slave population did all the work. Richer men bought up land and purchased slaves at auctions to farm it, putting the free men out of jobs. They also used their wealth to buy votes for candidates for high offices whom they wanted to see elected. As the rich got richer, the free poor became more and more debt-ridden.[1] They had little to do except hang about the streets or in taverns, arguing and brawling and drinking, easy prey to a new type of person, the political agitator, who exploited their aimlessness. Soon, the bolder spirits among these down-and-outs formed themselves into gangs and went about bullying and robbing senators, merchants, bankers, landowners, sometimes in broad daylight. The Senate was unable to stop them because it was filled with members who had got into it by using these hooligans to terrorize political opponents at election time. This lawlessness spread far beyond the walls of the capital. More gangs were formed in towns and in the countryside, and highway robbery became a regular and frightening feature

---

[1] There was, of course, a substantial middle class of shopkeepers, other traders, craftsmen and public works officials, whose fortunes varied according to the economic conditions of the republic.

of everyday life.

In 133 BC Tiberius Sempronius Gracchus was elected a tribune of the people. His father was of good plebeian stock, but his mother was the daughter of the great Scipio who had defeated Hannibal. Gracchus tried to do something to arrest the rot which was gradually enveloping the state. One way to get the poor off the streets – and so out of trouble – was to get them back to the land. The big rush to buy land had in a great many cases been in flat defiance of a long-standing law, of 377, which said that no one should own more than 500 jugera[1] of public land. So Gracchus introduced a bill in the assembly enabling the state to take back all land from these private buyers over and above the 500 jugera limit. This land was to be broken up into lots and given away as farms. Despite the most ferocious opposition, the bill was passed, and a commission was set up to supervize the confiscation and re-distribution.

The aristocracy could not stop the commission, nor could they touch Gracchus while he was in office, for, by ancient law, the person of the tribune of the people was held to be sacrosanct, that is, it was a capital crime to harm him. But no sooner had Gracchus' term of office expired than the aristocracy engineered a street riot in which he was cut down and slain. The commission, however, continued its work and did bring some measure of relief to the poor.

Eleven years later, Tiberius's brother Caius got himself elected tribune of the people, and he embarked upon a programme of reform that was far more revolutionary. He renewed his brother's land law. He chipped away at the Senate's privileges by taking away from them the sole right to be judges in trials of officials in the provinces charged with

---

[1] A jugerum was a Roman acre, about 5/8 of an acre as we know it today.

corruption or bad government. This right was given to the new middle class who were not in the senate, and in some cases at least corruption was exposed and punished. And he arranged that poor people should be allowed to buy a quantity of grain once a month from the state granary at nominal cost. This was the beginning of the practice of feeding an idle populace.

But when Caius tried to introduce a bill extending the right of citizenship of Rome to a number of the Italian allies, which meant, among other things, giving them a vote in the Roman elections, plebeians and patricians alike resisted. They were not going to share their exclusive privileges with outsiders, although they did not object to these outsiders fighting alongside them in the army. Rioting followed, and Caius committed suicide.

The removal of these two fearless and progressive brothers did not bring about any improvement in the political scene. From then on, rioting became more frequent and it was generally more violent. The Senate was unable, possibly on some occasions unwilling, to do anything about it. Elections were regularly accompanied by wholesale bribery of electors by candidates or their supporters, at which street fighting was organized on an almost professional scale, often resulting in loss of life, and in victory for the most unsuitable men. Many of these would later go on to govern provinces or command armies in the field and would display the same inefficiency that had characterized their terms of office as consuls or other magistrates.

Some of Rome's enemies took advantage of this dreadful internal disorder, and in the last years of the second century, Roman armies endured several humiliating defeats at the hands of two dangerous opponents, Jugurtha, king of Numidia in North Africa, and the hordes of German barbarians from north of the Alps, the Cimbri and the Teutones. Every general of senatorial rank who was sent out to lead a Roman army against them was defeated, usually in circumstances of ignominy, or worse, accepted heavy bribes to go away and not fight at all. One man sent out to Africa was Quintus Caecilius Metellus. He at least was unbribable, but he was unable to defeat Jugurtha decisively or to capture him. It fell to a man of the humblest origins, the son of a poor farmer from the small town of Arpinum, about sixty miles from Rome, to preserve the honour of Roman arms in Africa and to save the state itself from the barbarians. He was Caius Marius.

This extraordinary man had few advantages of upbringing or education. He did not talk much and when he did it was usually gruffly, even rudely. He knew little outside the life of a soldier. But he was strong and self-willed, fearless and capable of enduring the worst hardships that he expected his men to suffer. This made him an ideal leader of men. Above all, he was guided by an unshakeable belief in his own destiny. It was often related, in his later life, how as a young man he had been walking in the fields when there dropped from the sky an eagle's nest, right into the folds of his toga. In it were seven baby eaglets, chirping and scratching away. Soothsayers told his father that this meant Caius was destined to be the leading man in Rome on seven occasions. Whether Marius actually believed in this or not, he certainly repeated the story from time to time during his career in which he was seven times consul.

Now Marius was an officer on Metellus's staff in Numidia. But he was convinced that he, and he alone, could win the war. He was shrewd enough to realize that he would not stand a chance of getting command unless he could show that Metellus was incapable of doing the job. So, while he served

Metellus faithfully enough in the field, he kept up a correspondence with friends in Rome in which he constantly harped
upon Metellus' ineffectiveness. Eventually, when, despite one
or two tactical successes Metellus had failed to destroy or
capture Jugurtha, Marius offered himself as candidate for the
consulship for 107. His groundwork had been well prepared.
By a large majority the people in the assembly passed a special
decree appointing him consul and gave him command in
Africa. It was the first of the seven in the prophecy.

Marius defeated Jugurtha and brought the war to an end,
though it was one of his officers, the aristocrat Lucius Cornelius Sulla, who actually secured the person of the Numidian
king and brought him to Rome in chains. This was something
Marius could never overlook and the rivalry between him and
Sulla which stemmed from this was to dominate Roman
politics in later years, with the most terrible results. But for
the present, Marius was the hero of the day. He had justified
the people's belief in him as the military leader the country
needed. No sooner had he celebrated his triumph, however,
when news of an appalling defeat of Roman arms reached the
city. Nearly 80,000 Romans had been cut to pieces at a great
battle near Arausio, in Gaul, by the barbarian Cimbri. The
senatorial commander, Quintus Servilius Caepio, survived,
but when he came back to Rome there was no welcome at
the gates, nor thanks for not having despaired of the state, as
in the case of Varro after Cannae (page *31*). Caepio was
disgraced and his property was confiscated.

It was fortunate for Rome that Marius was free to take
command of what was left of the army, and by popular
decree he was appointed consul for the second time, for 104.
The people clearly appreciated the value of having the same
man in charge for a longer period than the normal twelve
months. It was also very fortunate that the barbarians did not

at once move against Italy, or they must have overwhelmed most if not all of it. The situation gave Marius the opportunity to introduce sweeping reforms which were to revolutionize the Roman army.

These reforms were a crucial turning point in Roman history.

When he was clearing up in North Africa, Marius had recruited men who had no property or even jobs from Rome and other towns. This was an important change, for up to then troops could only be raised among property owners, which in the majority of cases meant farmers. Three years later, when he was appointed consul for the purpose of getting the state prepared to face the Cimbri and the Teutones, Marius decided the time had come to put the army on a professional basis, and it was a good time to do it because the large number of citizens out of work who could swell the ranks of a new regular army would enable the farmers to stay at work on their land. The new army was thenceforth to consist largely of men who would serve for many years, until they reached retirement age.

The advantages of having a regular army are many and have been proved over and over again. They were many in second century BC Rome, but there was another side to the coin. When soldiers were ready to retire, how did you, the general, reward them? You promised them land. If there was enough to go round for an immediate hand-out, then all would be well, and you would not have disgruntled veterans clamouring for their just rewards. But if there was not, or if the Senate – as often happened – delayed passing the necessary legislation to make the land available, you would almost overnight find yourself with considerable political power, duty bound to press your veterans' claims.

It was this new phenomenon of the victorious general with

a large and loyal army behind him that was to become, time and again, the decisive factor in the political events in Rome for the next half century or so. And it led inexorably to the development of a new basis of government at Rome, military dictatorship of a permanent nature. Of all Caesar's titles, dictator perpetuus was the most apt to describe his real powers – and the one most galling to the starry-eyed republican senators who murdered him.

One clear sign of the way things were going was the ease with which Marius got himself elected consul for three years running, in 103, 102 and 101, to enable him to build up the army he thought would be necessary to deal with the bar-barian danger. It was against constitutional practice to be elected twice, let alone twice running. Three times in a row had never even been dreamed of. And a bourgeois, too! Such was the danger with which Rome was threatened. Such, too, was the implicit faith the state had in this rough, boorish, military genius. And the state's confidence was amply justified by two magnificent victories, over the Teutones at Aquae Sextiae in 102 and over the Cimbri at Vercellae the following year (see map). Marius returned to Rome and stood for the consulship for the sixth time. He was unbeatable!

Some years earlier – we do not know exactly when – Marius, the man of the people who never forgot his humble origins, had taken a wife – straight from the ranks of the aristocracy. She was Julia, daughter of C. Julius Caesar, of whom nothing is known except that he was a patrician of ancient lineage. This strange union must have been viewed with horror by the aristocrats who cannot have liked the way Marius used his new connections to advance his career. When he was the foremost man in the empire, there must have been many patricians who bitterly regretted his ascendancy, and they will not have been mollified by Marius' constant jibes at

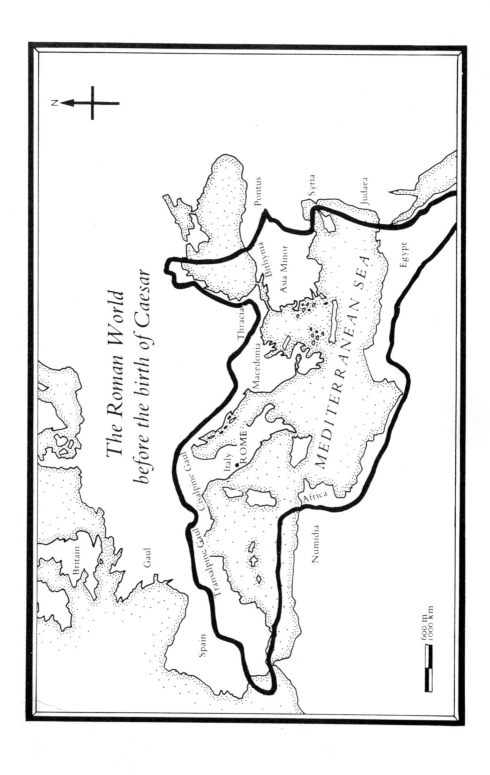

The Roman World
before the birth of Caesar

N

Britain

Gaul

Spain

Transalpine Gaul

Cisalpine Gaul

Italy

ROME

Macedonia

Thracia

Bithynia

Pontus

Asia Minor

Syria

Judaea

Egypt

MEDITERRANEAN SEA

Africa

Numidia

600 m
1000 km

their class for which, despite his marriage, he had only the utmost contempt.

Just about the time that Marius celebrated his triumph over the barbarians, his wife's brother, also called C. Julius Caesar, became a father. Down in a modest house in the bustling quarter of Rome called the Suburra, near the Esquiline Hill, and not far from the Forum, the centre of Roman life, Aurelia, his wife, gave birth to a son, on the 13th July, 100 BC. He was Caius Julius Caesar, and he was destined to become the greatest man in the world.

EARLY YEARS

Both sides of Caesar's family had noble ancestors, who had held high office. On his father's side a great-grandfather, Quintus Marcius Rex, was praetor in 144 BC. He claimed descent from the fourth king of Rome, Ancus Marcius (c. 642 – c. 617 BC), who had founded the sea-port town of Ostia on the mouth of the Tiber, some eighteen miles from the city. On his mother's side, several of the men had been consuls, including Lucius Aurelius Cotta, in 144, and his son (of the same name) in 119. And of course there was Marius. But in spite of this distinguished background, Caesar's parents were not at all well off, and they had a continuous struggle to maintain a standard of living befitting such ancestry and to bring up three children. Julius was the only son, but he had two sisters. One of these, Julia, was to become the grand-mother of the first emperor of Rome, Augustus, whom Caesar adopted at the end of his life, and whom we shall meet later on.

For centuries it has been said that Caesar was born by what we call Caesarian section, that is, the removal of a baby from his mother's womb by surgery, but there has never been any proof. The name Caesar might have come from the Latin word *caesus*, meaning cut, but if it did, then it will have been assumed by one of his ancestors. Romans of the upper class usually had at least three names. The first, the praenomen, was an individual name like Caius or Lucius or Quintus or Marcus, what we would call a Christian name. The second name was the nomen, which indicated the tribe or clan in which the child was born, such as the Julii or the Cornelii or the Licinii. These clans often had many members. A member used the name in the singular, such as Lucius *Cornelius* Sulla, or Marcus *Licinius* Crassus. The third name was the cognomen, which indicated the actual family in the clan, such as Caesar or Sulla or Scipio or Cato. Sometimes a fourth name called an agnomen might be added to mark a famous military exploit, and one of the best examples of this was that of Publius Cornelius Scipio *Africanus*, who defeated Hannibal in North Africa. The plebeians usually had only a praenomen and a nomen. Two great men who in one way or another made an impact on Caesar had only two names, Caius Marius and Quintus Sertorius.

Caesar was called Caius by his family and friends and Caesar by nearly everyone else. No one in 100 BC would have dreamed that the new baby would one day give his name to all the rulers of the Roman Empire, and, in adapted form, to the later rulers of Persia (Shah), Imperial Russia (Czar) and Imperial Germany (Kaiser).

In republican times, both parents took a close interest in their children's upbringing, even if there were slaves to do most of the household chores associated with it. In patrician homes, girls did not as a rule have much education, but boys were most carefully taught. They began by learning from slave tutors the Latin alphabet, which had 23 letters,[1] and went on

---

[1] They had no 'J' which was arrived at by using an 'I' in front of another vowel, or 'U', for which they used a 'V', or 'W'. The ancient Romans used only capital letters.

to simple reading. Then they tackled grammar and sentence construction, and built up a vocabulary. They also learned arithmetic, first using the fingers of both hands for counting and then getting to know the abacus, a board on which arithmetical sums were done by pushing counters, or *calculi*, along lines representing ten or multiples of ten.

When a boy was considered properly grounded in these elementary things, he would have a new tutor, either one who visited his house regularly or one who gave classes to select children of patrician parents in his house or elsewhere. These tutors were scholars who specialized in the Greek language, history, mythology and philosophy, for the Roman upper classes had by Caesar's childhood stopped regarding Greek culture as unworthy of attention.[1] Caesar was introduced to a new and very gifted tutor, at the age of about ten. This was Antonius Gnipho, a north Italian who had mastered Greek at the university at Alexandria, and who loved his job. For some years Caesar worked hard, studying the books of Homer, the tales of Aesop, the plays of Menander, the histories of Thucydides and Xenophon, as well as the works of the leading Latin authors. He learned how to express himself on paper and developed a distinctive style of writing, simple, pure, lucid and forceful, with which he wrote all his life. It is wonderfully shown in his books on his wars in Gaul and the civil wars (see page *184*). This grounding in writing was a prelude to the next stage of his education, the study of oratory. If you were going to get anywhere in public life in Rome, you had to be able to speak well in front of an audience. Whatever else many senators were not able to do properly, as we saw on page *36*, they could make good speeches before their colleagues in the Senate and on the Rostrum before the mob in the Forum, the

---

[1] Marius could never understand why they bothered to study the literature of a subject race, as the Greeks were.

central area of Roman business and political activity.

Caesar took to the study of Greek with relish, and he loved the history, the myths, the religion, the poetry, and the philosophy, especially of Plato and Aristotle. He longed to see Greece and he questioned his uncle Marius all about the buildings of Athens and Corinth, the ruins of Mycenae, but Marius had never really noticed them, for he had looked at Greece only as a military problem. Caesar wanted, too, to study at Rhodes in the world famous school of rhetoric. And this love of Greek culture stayed with him all of his life, so much that in his last days he thought seriously about moving the capital of the empire from Rome into the area of Greek civilization, to Alexandria, or Troy or Byzantium.

In these years of growing up, Caesar wrote a lot of poetry, tried his hand at a few short plays, and began to keep a note-book in which he jotted down wise and witty remarks he heard in the course of his life. He spent the best part of his time at study and in listening to his elders in the conversation which went on at dinner evening after evening in his home. But if you should think that Caesar was a 'swot', uninterested in mixing with other boys and girls of his own age, too soft to join in the athletics and games which most Roman children loved, you would be quite wrong. He was, despite delicate health from babyhood, a fast runner, had learned to fence well with short and long sword, and even as a boy handled a horse as skilfully as a trained cavalryman in the army. One trick which astonished even his uncle Marius was jumping on and off a horse or riding it at high speed, with his hands tied behind his back.

Caesar came of age when he was sixteen. A year earlier his father had died while out walking one day in the town of Pisa, and Caesar thereupon became head of the family. He was now surrounded by women, his mother Aurelia, his two

Roman theatre at Ostia, the port of Rome

sisters, his aunt Julia, and before long he became engaged.[1]

Coming of age meant taking on the toga virilis, the symbol of manhood. The toga was the Roman national costume. It was worn by Romans for centuries. Assuming it was a landmark in one's life. It was a large circle of white wool material, about three yards in diameter, which had to be draped over the body. The knack of doing this required some skill. It was a heavy garment and it often had to be adjusted during a busy day.[2] It lost its whiteness very quickly and so it had to be laundered frequently. This wore out the fabric which meant having a new one made. All the same, the toga was a garment 'worthy of the masters of the world, flowing, solemn, eloquent'. (Jerome Carcopino).

Caesar always wore his toga looser than other men. Perhaps it was when he first donned a toga that his care for the correctness of his attire began. Certainly from a very young age he drew attention to himself by his appearance. Romans used to wear, under the toga, a simple loin cloth of linen knotted round the waist, and over this a tunic (a kind of long shirt) of wool or linen, fastened by a sash. It was short sleeved, but Caesar's always had long sleeves with fringes. This bother about his appearance went beyond his clothes. Like most Romans of his time he had his chin shaved by a barber every morning and his hair trimmed, but he was particularly fussy about his hair, ordering the barber to pull out odd hairs with tweezers, so that nothing was out of place. But, dandy though he was, it was not a sign of effeminacy or inordinate concern for trivial things. It was much more a manifestation of his deep desire for order and harmony, which underlay everything that he did.

[1] To a girl of plebeian stock, Cossutia. He broke the engagement to marry Cornelia, daughter of L. Cornelius Cinna in 84.

[2] When Caesar was stabbed and knew he was dying, he unfolded his toga to allow part to fall over his feet, so that the whole body was covered.

A statue of Gaius Marius in his later years. It gives a good idea of how a toga was worn.

When he was 16, Caesar had reached his full height of about 5 ft. 8 ins., tall for a Roman. Behind his unconventional dress he was an extremely good-looking young man, of fine proportions, his head especially remarkable for the harmony of its features. Most noticeable were his very dark eyes, luminous and rivetting. In later years Caesar is reported to have once quelled a mutiny of the 10th Legion with one word. Could it have been that the ringleaders were transfixed by the powerful glare of his flashing eyes?

At this time, too, Caesar began to follow avidly the proceedings in the Senate, where business of state was done and whither reports of activities on the outskirts of the empire were delivered by messenger or in person by officials. He soon grasped the calamitous position into which the republic had been sinking, for he was living through the disordered days of the feud between his uncle Marius and Sulla, the war between the Romans and their Italian allies, and the bloodthirsty attacks on Roman officials in Asia by the brutal and swaggering Mithradates VI, king of Pontus.

When Marius came home after his second great victory against the barbarians, at Vercellae, in 101, he was yet again elected consul, now for the sixth time. He believed it was an expression of the country's thanks. And so it was, but only in part, for those who voted out of gratitude also voted because they hoped he would, with his great reputation, put an end to the political disorders affecting the whole Roman way of life.

As we have seen, the patricians (or aristocracy as we would term them) had been having things their own way in the government of Rome and the empire for a long time. Their majority in the Senate was so big that any senator who did not support them was usually unlikely to make much headway in an official career. This majority came to be lumped together under the collective word, the Optimates, which is really another word for aristocrats. They were bent on maintaining things as they were, regardless of how unsatisfactory, on keeping the selection of officials for government and imperial posts in their hands. They could even fix the results of elections the way they wanted them by using bribery and they practised this on a massive scale. They had engineered the deaths of the two able and reforming Gracchi brothers who had opposed them (page 35) and they had devised a new formula for strengthening their grip on the Senate, as they imagined for ever. This was the 'ultimate decree', an arrangement whereby if they thought their authority was in serious danger from any source, they could order the consuls in office to 'see to it that the state comes to no harm'. This gave the consuls power to banish – or put to death, if need be – any politician in or outside the senate who might try to curb their powers.

Those who opposed them in – and more numerously outside – the senate were the Populares. This party label covered a mixed bag of Romans, some of whom belonged to the equestrian class,[1] rich young sons of senators who liked playing with revolution (there were several of these), plebeians of good stock who were keen to reform the evils of the system. They were outwardly keen on giving more power to the people, which was really taking it away from the Optimates. Inwardly, however, many of the leaders were more interested in building themselves into an effective alternative power group in the republic. Their principal representatives were the tribunes of the people (see glossary).

One of the tribunes for the year 100, L. Appuleius Saturninus, an associate of Marius, put forward a programme of reform. It included proposals for land allotments as rewards for Marius's victorious troops. This land was not to be in Italy but in provinces such as Cisalpine Gaul and North Africa, and it was to be given to Romans and allied troops alike. The qualification for an allotment was a certified period of service in Marius's army.

On the whole, the proposals seemed fair enough, but they provoked the most bitter opposition from the Optimates who saw in it a precedent whereby, in future, a general could bind an army to his cause and even threaten the state itself. To get the measures through, moreover, Marius and Saturninus used unconstitutional methods. They brought the measures to the Assembly which passed them. This was all right, but Saturninus had added a clause which compelled the Senate to swear an oath to abide by the measures, but it was so framed that the Senate, in swearing, would be promising to acknowledge any

---

[1] The equestian class represented the material interests in Rome, that is, bankers, moneylenders, tax-collectors (who earned commission). They also represented families with wealth but who had no history of holding any of the magistracies.

measures put forward during Marius' consulship as legal, even
if they were not. So the Optimates resisted. At the next
elections, Saturninus and a colleague, Glaucia, who was
running for consul, hired some thugs to murder the Optimates' candidate for the consulship, Memmius. Rioting
followed, and Saturninus was killed by a gang employed by
the Optimates. The Senate then issued the ultimate decree and
instructed the consul, Marius, to take action to save the state
and arrest Glaucia and his followers. Marius captured them
and probably promised that they should come to no harm.
But more Optimate bullies seized them and put them to death,
it is said, by pelting them with clay tiles from the roof of the
senate house.

It was the end of the Saturnine episode; it was also the finish
of Marius as a politician. By agreeing to carry out the decree
he had betrayed the Populares. Many of their other leaders
were dead. Their struggle for power seemed doomed.

Over the next ten years many attempts were made to re-
structure the political system of the republic, but they were all
frustrated by the Optimates. Then, in 91, M. Livius Drusus,
one of the tribunes, who was an Optimate, introduced a fresh
set of proposals in the Senate, including reform of the law
courts and extending Roman citizenship to the Italian allies.
The Italians had long sought – and deserved – the privilege.
They had formed the backbone of Marius' armies. But the
Optimates blocked the proposal and, worse, engineered the
assassination of Drusus one dark night just as he was opening
the front door of his home. It was the story of the Gracchi
brothers all over again.

The death of Drusus led to something Romans had been
dreading for years. Deprived of yet another chance to get
citizenship, the Italians decided to fight for it. At Asculum a
Roman magistrate and several businessmen were murdered.

Within days the Italian tribes all over the peninsula flocked to arms and before many weeks they had an army of over 100,000 men. Rome was surrounded by hostile tribes everywhere, except in Etruria and Latium. Would the Optimates finally take the blinkers away from their eyes and give the Italians the citizenship they craved?

They did, but not before more than a year of the most bitter fighting[1] up and down the country had robbed both sides of hundreds of thousands of good men. Both Marius and Sulla commanded armies which won victories, but to no avail if the Italians were still to be deprived, pledged as they were to fight to the last man. In 89 the Senate finally agreed to laws admitting to citizenship all allies who surrendered within sixty days. The Samnites alone held out, ancient enemies of Rome, who in recent years had only stayed quiet through lack of opportunities of taking revenge for grievances going back hundreds of years. It fell to Sulla to bring them to heel, and when he had, the war was over. Well it was over, too, and the Italians' demands granted, for terrible news had reached an exhausted Rome. Mithradates VI, king of Pontus in Asia Minor, had invaded Roman Asia and slaughtered 80,000 Italian-born emigrants who had made their lives out there. And all Greece was in revolt.

The Senate appointed the consul, Sulla, to command an expeditionary force to Asia. Sulla was about fifty. An Optimate, whose family had not been wealthy, he was in the prime of life. Thickset, fair haired, with piercing blue eyes, he had made his way to the highest office by a mixture of courage, diplomatic skill, ruthlessness, and the ability to wait for the right moment to move up the ladder. He already had a reputation for handling troops well, getting the best out of

[1] A struggle known as the Social Wars because it was fought between Romans and their allies (socii) in Italy.

them in the most adverse situations. Now he prepared to take a Roman army out to Asia.

Suddenly, the Populares found a new leader who was determined, as a first show of power, to get Sulla's command revoked and transferred to Marius, who was nearly seventy. This was the Optimate, P. Sulpicius Rufus, one of the most famous orators of his age. In 88 BC he was elected tribune, but at once deserted the Optimates and introduced a series of measures aimed at crippling the power of the Senate. Among these was one to disqualify anyone from being a senator if they were in debt. This would effectively have removed a considerable number of Optimates who had for long been living beyond their means and were heavily mortgaged. The Senate called upon Sulla to block the proposals. Sulla walked down to the Assembly and was mobbed. Sensing that his life was in danger his officers managed to get him away to a house nearby – which belonged to Marius! It was a dramatic moment for both men, Sulla the consul having to beg sanctuary with Marius, his arch-enemy, still the hero of the Populares. Marius could have put an end to his rival then and there – and possibly have averted the terrible bloodshed which was to follow in the next years, but instead the old general released him. Within a few weeks he was bitterly to regret this clemency.

Sulla set off at once to join his army which was waiting near Capua. Sulpicius, meanwhile, appealed to the Assembly to invest Marius with Sulla's command in Asia, and immediately he secured their approval he sent messengers to Sulla with orders to hand over the command. Sulla's response was to laugh – and to clap the messengers in irons. His army had been expecting to march to Brundisium to embark in transports for Greece. Imagine their horror when Sulla ordered them to turn and march with him against Rome, their city, centre of the empire they and their forebears had helped to create! It was unprecedented, and it added a new and terrifying dimension to the violent political scene in the capital. But, cajoled with bribes and promises of rich rewards in cash, corn and land, they marched.

Inside the city few preparations had been made to resist Sulla. Marius took charge and gave a lot of orders, but there were hardly any soldiers to carry them out. Advance troops of Sulla's reached the Esquiline Gate and broke in, setting fire to the roofs of the houses on the way to stop the defenders using them. Marius realized that the city had no chance and he gave the word to scatter. Many of the leaders of the Populares were caught and executed on the spot. One was Sulpicius whose head was exhibited on a spike in the Forum. Marius got away with some followers, and they were all outlawed.

The escapers headed for Ostia and took to sea. But a gale drove them ashore, and Marius had to spend the night in a wood without food or shelter. The next morning they set off down the coast, Marius keeping their spirits up by recalling the prophecy of the seven eaglets (see page *37*) and reminding them that he had been consul six times. A few days later they reached Minturnae and fell into the arms of the local police. Marius was locked up in a dark cell while the authorities deliberated what to do with him. Then they sent in a warrior of the Cimbri tribe (which he had crushed at Vercellae in 101) with a sharp sword. As the warrior advanced and raised his arms to strike, the old man glowered at him and yelled out 'Man, do you dare to kill Caius Marius?' The Cimbrian ran from the room crying at the top of his voice 'I can't kill Caius Marius!'

So the authorities let Marius go and gave him a ship in which to sail to North Africa. He landed at Carthage, but there had to endure another humiliation. The resident governor ordered him to leave. Marius replied to the messenger: 'Tell

A Roman war galley. This is the kind of ship that might have been used in the Aegean Sea during Thermus' campaign against the Mytileneans.

the governor you have seen Caius Marius, a fugitive, sitting amid the ruins of Carthage!'

Back in Rome Sulla had carried out a swift programme of legislation aimed to ensure that Rome would be governed by the senate in his absence. He was in a hurry to get off to Asia where Mithradates was doing all he could to unite everyone in the East against Rome. No sooner had Sulla reached Greece when Rome was rent by more revolution. The two consuls, L. Cornelius Cinna and Cn. Octavius, fell out over a bill to put the new Italian citizens of Rome on the same footing as the old. When the bill was put to the Assembly by Cinna, the Optimates, led by Octavius, made an armed attack on Cinna and his supporters and drove them out of the city. A new consul was appointed in Cinna's place, without the procedure of an election. It was unconstitutional but the Optimates had long ceased to worry about formalities if they thought their interests benefitted without them.

Cinna had little difficulty in raising an army to restore his position, and he sent a message to Marius in Africa inviting him to return. And so the old man did, with a small picked force of Italian supporters, but it was not the Marius who had left a year or so earlier. Humiliated, bitter, and increasingly out of control of his passions through long bouts of drinking, he had not cut his hair since the day he left Rome and it now reached his waist. Filled with a desire for revenge, he returned to the city walls insisting on the declaration of outlawry being officially revoked, before he would enter. And as he waited outside the gates for the Assembly to move the resolution, he began to think of everyone in Rome who he thought had wronged him. The Assembly hurriedly met and formally cancelled his exile. He came into the city and shut the gates. The most frightful scenes followed. The old man, consumed with vengeance, aggravated by drink, staggered down the

streets, accompanied by a band of fellow exiles armed with
swords and daggers. Every time he pointed his finger at someone in the road his accomplices rushed forward and stabbed
him. Many had come out of their homes to welcome him, but
this did not save them if he imagined they had once wronged
him. Naturally, Octavius fell, and so did many of the Senate.
But in his blind rage the old man actually signalled the death
of two relatives of Caesar, and of his, and before anyone could
stop them, the gangs had struck. Marius' fury frightened even
Cinna and his friends. So they engineered his election as consul
for the seventh time, thus fulfilling the prophecy, in the hope
that the honour would stay his hand. It did not, but less than
two weeks after taking office, Marius collapsed from an attack
of pleurisy and died almost at once, at the end of January, 86.
All Rome sighed with relief. The reign of terror was at an end.

For the next three years, Cinna virtually ruled Rome. He
held the consulship with carefully chosen friends for three
years running, and in that time introduced many forward-
looking measures. But his rule was unstable, for news began
to come through of great victories won by Sulla over Mithradates. Many of the Optimates who put up with Cinna's
government did so because they believed Sulla would return
and settle once and for all that Rome was to be governed by
the Senate. And so it happened. In 84, Cinna was murdered
in a mutiny among the troops. At the same moment, having
defeated him several times in the field, Sulla negotiated a peace
treaty with Mithradates, and prepared to return to Rome for
a well-earned triumph for himself and rewards for his
victorious soldiers. Once more, the city was faced with the
prospect of a Roman general leading an army against it.

What happened to Caesar during these awful times, the
background to which must be grasped if one is to understand
what motivated him in his later years? As the nephew of

Marius and the relative of several men holding high office, he saw events at first hand and he got to know the leading personalities. During the last days of his uncle's reign of terror, Marius had recommended Caesar for a vacancy in the priesthood, a considerable honour for one so young. Two years later, when he was sixteen, Caesar, who had met and fallen in love with Cornelia, the daughter of Cinna, married her. He thus became the son-in-law of the greatest man in Rome. But within months Cinna lost his life and the situation in Rome was altered. Sulla was on his way home, and it was known that he, like Marius, had a list of scores to settle. Anyone who had had anything to do with the Populares or Marius or Cinna was in the utmost danger. Young Caesar was no exception.

Sulla entered Rome in 82 and at once embarked upon reconstructing the constitution. His settlement was based on restoring to the senate nearly all of its old powers. To get his laws through he had himself appointed dictator as well as holding the consulship for three years. He fortified the Senate by enlarging its membership and giving it control of law-making and the law courts. This meant drastically cutting down the powers and rights of the Assembly and the tribunes of the people who were no longer allowed to introduce any bills without the senate's consent. Nor were they qualified to stand for the consulship.

While he was regulating the new order, Sulla also acted out his vengeance. But unlike the massacres of Marius which at least had the virtue of being political insecurity aggravated by drink and rage, Sulla calmly and cold-bloodedly wrote out and published a full list of those whom he regarded as public enemies. These lists, or proscriptions, as they came to be called, were posted in the Forum for all to see, and they were death-warrants for those who did not immediately take the hint and leave the country. Nearly 1700 names appeared in a string of lists posted over a few days; forty senators and over sixteen hundred equites were outlawed, with a price on every head. Their property was confiscated and their children and grandchildren were excluded from Roman citizenship. On top of this some 3000 Samnite prisoners, taken from an army which had resisted his march on Rome, were butchered in the Circus Maximus one morning when Sulla was addressing the Senate. The screams and groans of the victims could be heard above his words, but his cold indifference to horrors is well illustrated by the fact that he continued with his speech as if nothing was occurring. The tomb of Marius was opened up and the great man's ashes were scattered, and all the monuments and trophies of his victories were cast down.

Among those who were considered for revenge was Caesar. Blameless enough though he was, he was the lawful husband of Cinna's daughter. Sulla decided to spare his life but requested him to divorce Cornelia and take another wife from the Optimate party. To his astonishment, Caesar refused. He was in love with Cornelia and he was not going to make her or himself unhappy. Now Sulla always admired pluck; he also appreciated that no good could come from making a martyr of a nineteen-year-old member of the priesthood. When influential members of Caesar's family begged Sulla to forgive the boy's bravado, he relented, but he told them: 'Beware of this young man. He wears his belt like a girl but in his heart there is more than one Marius.'

Sulla was cold, calculating and unflappable, but he was also, by contrast, very superstitious. Did he detect in the young man some sign of future greatness, at the time quite invisible to anyone else, including Caesar?

Caesar was no doubt as amazed at his good fortune as Sulla had been at his impudence. But he was wise enough not to take any further risks, and he prepared to leave Rome for a more healthy atmosphere. He had already decided to go into politics. A necessary first step was to serve in the army abroad, and in 80 he was posted to the staff of the new governor of Asia, M. Minucius Thermus. Apart from anything else, this would give Caesar the chance to see Greek civilization in the lands of its origins. It must have been a thrilling moment for him when the ship set sail for Greece.

FIRST STEPS TO POWER

Caesar was now twenty. He already had wisdom and commonsense, and his upbringing in a climate of almost unrelieved violence had instilled in him a realism that was to distinguish him throughout his life. Indeed it often separated him from many of his contemporaries. Caesar had also learned to dissimulate, and it is possible that these qualities recommended him to Thermus who, almost as soon as Caesar reached Asia sent him on an important mission to the king of Bithynia, Nicomedes IV, a cultivated monarch who was an ally of Rome. Thermus, who was out to punish the Mytileneans for their part in supporting Mithradates, needed some of his ships to help blockade the city of Mytilene. Although the king had promised his aid, the governor was not inclined to rely upon the word of the Asiatic whose allegiance was tenuous.

So Caesar was entrusted with the job of persuading Nicomedes to send his ships and seeing that they embarked before the crafty king could change his mind. But when they met, Caesar and Nicomedes immediately took to each other, and the king, who enjoyed enormous wealth and whose court was luxurious but nonetheless tasteful, entertained him in the most lavish manner. Some Roman businessmen who were present at one of the banquets regarded the intimacy of Caesar and this oriental king as evidence of a homosexual relationship. When they got back to Rome they spread the story about, and before long Caesar was being talked about as the 'queen' of Bithynia. It was taken up by most Roman historians, whether for or against him. But those who did repeat the story – which was re-iterated with great gusto at his triumphs of 46 BC, some 35 years later – also took the trouble to tell how Caesar won the highest award for an individual act of gallantry in battle.

He had persuaded Nicomedes to send the fleet, and when Thermus laid siege to Mytilene, Caesar was right at the forefront of the attack, leading a detachment of commandoes against the city walls. At this moment he saved one of his men's life, though we do not know how.

The siege was successful and the city surrendered. Thermus decorated Caesar with the Civic Crown, the highest award for bravery that the Romans could bestow. It could be worn on every festive occasion. If he appeared in any public games, everyone would stand up and cheer. He could sit in the Senate to hear the senators making speeches. It was the first time Caesar demonstrated his immense personal courage. There were to be many more.

Once the Mytileneans had been overcome, Thermus gave Caesar an administrative post in the government of Asia. Although it was a junior one, it gave Caesar the chance to see how Roman colonial administration worked, what were the defects, and how easy it was to make money out of the natives by exploiting them.

In 78, news came through from Rome that Sulla had died at his villa at Puteoli, hardly a year after abdicating the dictatorship. To Caesar this was a great relief. It was now safe to go back home, for since Sulla had proscribed so many families, those who were in power after his death were not likely to continue the persecutions. And so it proved, for when he returned to a happy welcome by his wife, Cornelia, his daughter Julia, and his mother and family, he found a strong movement of opinion in the city wanting to reverse the Sullan constitution. It was led by Marcus Aemilius Lepidus, one of the consuls. He was courting the support of the remnants of the Marian party who remained in Rome. The greater part of the Marians, however, had fled to Spain to join Sertorius (see page 68).

As soon as he heard that Caesar had come back, Lepidus sought to enlist his support. But Caesar, despite his anxiety to see his uncle's party rise again, instantly assessed Lepidus' capabilities and believed they were not of the calibre that could effectively overthrow the Sullan order and build a new one. So, for his own good he decided to stay out of politics for a while and concentrate on the next stage in his career, advocacy in the Roman courts. In the meantime he took up his interests, poetry, plays, history, and he began to attack a new one, science. He also began to make a name for himself as a giver of good parties. He made friends among all sorts of people, friends whom he chose with some care, who might help him in his career. Among these were men of wealth from whom he began to borrow money. The most prominent of these was Marcus Licinius Crassus. And he took care to see that these friends were people who believed, as he did, that the constitution had to be restructured. The Lepidus movement, as he anticipated, failed because it was not properly planned, and because it had not offered, as an essential bait, the restoration of the powers of the tribunes.

In those days, one of the quickest ways to make your mark in the political arena when you were young was to prosecute

Possibly the bust of Brutus, one of the chief assassins of Caesar

in an important criminal trial. The opportunities in this were frequent, because so many governors and commanders in the provinces exploited the natives under their protection and accepted bribes for a variety of favours. Every year men came back to Rome to find themselves arraigned on charges of extortion or corruption while in office. It was a legitimate exercise for a young and aspiring advocate to pursue.

In 76 Caesar decided to prosecute Cn. Cornelius Dolabella, who had governed Macedonia from 80 to 78, for extortion. In doing so he showed his hand as a supporter of the Marian party, for Dolabella's appointment had been a Sullan one. There was little defence. Even Dolabella's friends were shocked by his greed. But he was able to brief the two leading orators of the day, Quintus Hortensius and Caius Cotta (Caesar's cousin), and despite his guilt they persuaded the judges to acquit. Caesar had lost his first case, but all the historians agree that his handling of the prosecution was masterly, and it left the public in little doubt that the senate's judges were corrupt.

A year later Caesar tried again, and this time it was on behalf of some Greeks who had been scandalously plundered by the proconsul, Caius Antonius Hybrida, the uncle of Caesar's later friend, Mark Antony. Again he had an excellent case and this time he won, in the courts, but Antonius got the verdict set aside by appealing to the tribunes. Although everyone who counted reassured him that his handling of both cases was excellent for one so young, and congratulated him on his fearlessness in prosecuting two staunch Sullans, Caesar felt he had a lot more to learn about oratory, and he decided to go to Rhodes to study under Apollonius Molo, the great teacher who had already been instructing Cicero, a contemporary young lawyer also determined to get to the top of the administrative tree.

So Caesar set out from Rome again for the East, but he was not to reach Rhodes without incident. As his ship approached the island of Pharmacussa, south of Miletus, in Asia Minor, it was attacked by pirates who drove it ashore. Caesar was taken, and the pirates demanded about £12,000 for his life. When he heard this, Caesar laughed loudly: 'I am worth at least £30,000' he said, proudly, and at once sent some of his colleagues off to Miletus to collect the ransom. In the meanwhile, Caesar remained captive for about six weeks, and in that time he endeared himself to the pirates by his boldness and his apparently total disregard for his own safety. When they stayed up late at night singing songs, dancing and banging drums and other instruments, he would send down messages ordering them to keep quiet. During the day he joined them in athletic contests and soon showed his superiority. He chided them for drinking too much. Then he would make them sit down and listen while he read them some of his verses. If they fidgetted or giggled, he rated them for not paying attention. From time to time he would tell them 'When I get free I'll come back and crucify the lot of you' – and they laughed all the more.

But they stopped laughing when a few weeks later the ransom was paid. He went to Miletus and raised a force with which he returned to the island and took the pirates by surprise when they were sleeping off some heavy banquet. He had got to know their habits well. Although he was as good as his word, he ordered their throats to be cut before the pirates were crucified.

Caesar went on to Rhodes where he spent several months studying under Apollonius. He was determined to improve his speaking and his argument construction, but at that moment he heard that Mithradates of Pontus had broken his treaty with Rome. So he abandoned his studies and returned to the mainland of Asia. There he raised an army of his own, took on an advance party of the king's forces and drove them out of the province. He did so quite without the authority of the governor, P. Servilius Vatia, but the boldness and the success of his attack outweighed the indiscipline, and the fact that he was the holder of the Civic Crown may have been why he got away with it.

At this point, he heard from his family in Rome that his cousin, Caius Cotta, had died. This Cotta was a pontifex, that is, he had a seat on the board of the college of priests, who were all men of high birth. The pontifex's role in Roman life was important and it carried political influence. Caesar's family used its influence to get him nominated to the vacancy and without much difficulty they succeeded. He came back to Rome in 74 to take up his seat. He had already decided to show his hand, and he plunged into the political fray, associating himself with the Populares, supporting the measures designed to uproot the Sullan order.

In the letter telling him about Cotta's death his family probably put him in the picture about the general political scene at Rome, and they may have hinted to him of the growing restlessness among all classes. Added to this was the gossip he picked up from Roman traders and visitors to Asia, and you may imagine that Caesar had a pretty gloomy idea of what he would find when he got home. No sooner had he returned when his worst fears were confirmed. Vast numbers of idle people were starving in the streets because the transports carrying the grain for the free hand-out to them were being captured one after the other by pirates like those who captured him. The slave population in the countryside was becoming extremely restive. A great many owners had been behaving with frightful cruelty to these unfortunates whose only crime in most cases was that they had been on the losing side in one war or another with Rome. Rebellion was imminent; the slaves only needed leadership, and this they were soon to get.

The Optimates, who had had their powers strengthened by Sulla, had proved beyond redemption that they could not manage. Every other Roman would have told Caesar, if he had asked them, that they were against the Senate, and some even would have sympathized with Rome's enemies. Out in Spain was an offshoot of the Marian party, led by a splendid soldier–statesman, Quintus Sertorius. This man, of humble birth, had risen to become praetor and governor of Spain, in 83. When Sulla took Rome in 82, many of the surviving Marians fled to Spain to join Sertorius who had, for the good of the empire, decided to set up an alternative government. He had even created a separate senate. Now, on his return to Rome, Caesar found that Sertorius had added immensely to his reputation by defeating every army sent against him by Rome. What is more, a large sector of the Marian party in Rome was secretly behind him. It was hoped Sertorius would one day come back to the city and re-structure the tottering republic. It would have seemed to an outsider a matter of amazement that the state could survive at all under these conditions.

Perhaps it was at this point that Caesar first began to think seriously about taking a major part in the reform work needed. He looked about him and sized up the present leadership, and more pertinently, the younger men with whom he would be working and competing. There were many, but the most promising three were Gnaeus Pompeius Magnus, Marcus Licinius Crassus, and Marcus Tullius Cicero. The fortunes of all three were in some way or other bound up with his.

Gnaeus Pompeius Magnus, known to history as Pompey, was about six years older than Caesar. Good-looking, courageous, a great general and an excellent leader of men, he was inordinately vain. As a politician he was hopelessly out of his depth among the masters of intrigue and double-dealing who dominated the senate. But almost to the end of his life he commanded the reverence of the army and of large sectors of the ordinary people who thought of him as another Alexander the Great. When Sulla came back to Italy in 82, Pompey was sent to Africa and Sicily to round up the Marian resistance, and he did so with great speed and efficiency. When he came to Rome Sulla greeted him as Magnus, or The Great. After Sulla's death he was regarded as one of the republic's foremost generals, and in 76 he was sent to Spain to help in the war against Sertorius, in whom, however, he more than met his match. In five years he was never able to defeat the great exile, and when Sertorius was finally destroyed it was by treachery at the dinner table and not in battle.

Marcus Licinius Crassus was an Optimate by birth, and he supported Sulla in the march on Rome. Crassus from an early age had two consuming ambitions, to make a fortune and to become a popular hero. He certainly succeeded with the first, but he never captured the love of the people. His earliest big step in money-making almost dropped into his lap. He had proved a good field commander in Sulla's fight for Rome in 82 and the dictator rewarded him by enabling him to purchase the confiscated properties of the proscribed families of the Populares. He turned these into money and used it well. He bought hundreds of slaves, spent fortunes in educating them in all manner of crafts and skills. He bought silver mines, farms, block of flats and tenement houses, and all were worked with the thoroughness of a modern city tycoon. They brought him immense wealth, enough, as he said, to maintain a complete army, and no one could be a leader if they could not do this. For a generation he was the richest man in Rome. He even

Portrait bust of Marcus Tullius Cicero, who was the greatest orator Rome ever produced. He could never bring himself to agree with Caesar's ideas on how the state should be governed, but the two men were always friends.

controlled the city's fire services. There was a story that if a house caught fire, Crassus would bring up his fire fighting carts to the front door and then put a proposition to the owner. Sell the house now and I'll pay the top price, whereupon if the deal was done, he sent the fire engines in. If you don't sell, I'll stop the firemen and let it burn down. Then I'll buy the land! Apart from his financial wizardry, Crassus was no mean general, and has probably been underrated.

Marcus Tullius Cicero came from comparatively humble beginnings. But even as a boy he loved everything to do with the Senate, its ranks, patricians and so on, to the extent that he would not – or perhaps could not – see the glaring deficiencies of the upper classes as a management structure for Rome. He entered public life as a lawyer and soon made his name as a leading orator. He, like Caesar, had studied under

Apollonius Molo. In 77 he came back to Rome and devoted several years to pleading causes before the courts.

He appeared as prosecutor against several provincial governors accused of corruption. He worked his way steadily up the career ladder, standing as it were on the fence between the Optimates and the Populares. For instance, he spoke in 66 BC in favour of the Manilian law giving Pompey command in the Near East against Mithradates (page *80*), a law passed by the Assembly. But when he achieved the consulship two years later he came down on the side of the Optimates. His love for the republic dominated everything. He believed the republic would be improved by those better elements within the Senate and even outside, whom he grouped together as the 'boni' or the 'good men'.

These three were to be Caesar's colleagues, rivals, friends, and all were to die violently.

The most important objective of the Populares was the restoration of the rights and powers of the tribunes of the people, which had been reduced to a minimum by Sulla. The first steps in undoing this work were achieved by a successful bill allowing tribunes to stand for the other offices of state. This was engineered in 75 by the C. Cotta whose death had brought Caesar home in 73. In that year he took an active part in the three-year campaign for the restoration of the rights, in particular the power to veto, that is, stop for a year, any measure passed by the Senate.

The political troubles in Rome, however, were swept into the background by the eruption of a most dangerous revolt among the slave population, late in 73. Led by one Spartacus, a Thracian bandit who had been sold to a school for gladiators at Capua, about seventy slaves and gladiators escaped from the school and raised the standard of revolt. Within days the news spread like wildfire among the slave population throughout Italy and when a few weeks later, Spartacus led a force against a Roman commander and defeated it, the bulk of the slaves rose up and joined him. For two years he defeated every Roman army sent against him, and ravaged Italy far and wide. Finally, in 71, another army was sent out under Crassus who defeated Spartacus, captured him, and crucified him, along with his henchmen. Pompey, meanwhile, who had returned from Spain, mopped up the remnants of the revolt in the south, and between them, Crassus and Pompey returned to Rome to receive the thanks of the state for having saved it. At this point Caesar played one of his critical roles in Roman history, one requiring the utmost diplomacy and patience.

Now Crassus and Pompey had been at loggerheads for years. It was not just that they were two very different people. Ever since the capture of Rome by Sulla, Pompey had been the more favoured commander and had been in the limelight most of the time. And yet Crassus had been as helpful to Sulla, and in 82 at least there was nothing to say who was the better commander. Here were grounds for jealousy and distrust, and all the wealth that Crassus had accumulated could not assuage his envy, this man who loved money but who coveted a military reputation. When the two men came towards Rome, everyone waited to see what honours they received and how they would take them. The Senate decided that Pompey should receive a triumph for his success in Spain, but Crassus only an ovation because his war had been against slaves. The difference was not a very great one. But it was the most tactless thing the Senate could have done at this time.

Pompey and Crassus had built their careers on Sulla's triumphs. The Senate could have looked to them as two staunch supporters, and now in 71 both men had armies behind them. If they could have been persuaded to bury their differences and join together to act as military back-up for the

Senate's programme of government, such as it was, the Optimates would have been unassailable, possibly for many years. Admittedly, Crassus had some minor grievances against the Senate, for the most part over financial matters, but Pompey had nothing to complain about at all.

The lesser honour for Crassus turned his grievance into an angry resentment. Caesar was quick to appreciate how this could be used to the advantage of the popular party which was still clamouring for the full restoration of the tribunes' powers. He was on good terms with Pompey. He had known Crassus for years and was already deeply in debt to him financially. So he negotiated with both men and succeeded in doing what the Senate had not even attempted, got them to work together. Both men announced their candidatures for the consulship for 70. Crassus was qualified, as he had come up by the conventional ladder. Pompey was not, but with two armies outside the city gates and their leaders seemingly united and ready to use them, the Senate had to yield and allow Pompey to stand. They announced that the first thing they would do was restore the powers of the tribunes.

The elections were a foregone conclusion. The tribunate was freed from its Sullan shackles. The law courts were removed from the sole control of the Senate. And, as if to deal a death-blow to Sulla's senate, the office of censor was revived. Censors were responsible for the census of the Roman population and they kept a check on the credentials of members of the Senate. Periodically, they reported that certain members should be expelled, for one or other of a variety of reasons, generally associated with corruption or inefficiency. Now, the censors dismissed over sixty senators and among these was that Antonius Hybrida whom Caesar had prosecuted in 75. To the immense relief of the whole city, a revolution had taken place quietly, efficiently and without bloodshed, and men started to look forward to better times.

They were to be disappointed. The whole basis of the new order depended upon the continuation of the working together of Crassus and Pompey, and neither man was big enough to forget his differences. The next ten years of Roman history were greatly influenced by the state of the relations between these two men, and not a little of Caesar's time was spent trying to heal the wounds and damp down the ever simmering antagonism. The Senate, meanwhile, perfectly aware of the situation, did its best to aggravate it.

The year 70 was an eventful one for Romans. Apart from the big legislation programme which kept the Senate and the Assembly occupied for several weeks, there were the preparations leading up to Pompey's triumph, the actual triumph itself, and a series of enormous banquets organized by Crassus at which tables for 10,000 guests were laid out for one sitting. These banquets were a desperate attempt by Crassus to court popularity, but once the effects of over-eating and too much wine had worn off and men had got back to their everyday business, they forgot the banquets and remembered only how the handsome Pompey, in full triumphal dress, had given them one of the greatest entertainments in their lives.

Towards the end of the year, the annual elections for the next year's magistracies arrived, and Caesar stood for one of the quaestorships. There were twenty elected each time, and they were deputies to consuls and praetors in Rome or in provinces. Their principal duty was the administration of financial affairs, and the office entitled them to a seat in the senate. There must have been many people who chuckled when Caesar won a quaestorship, with a posting to Further Spain as financial secretary to the governor. By then he was already notorious as a big spender and was up to his ears in debt. Rumour had it that he owed well over £1,000,000 in the money of today. Much of this was to Crassus who believed in him and who regarded the money as an investment, for there was much more for Caesar to do to help him. Caesar indulged his taste for beautiful things, works of art, and chose them with care. There was never any doubt about their quality or their cost – both were of the highest order. He is said to have had a luxurious country house built on Lake Nemi, only to have it demolished almost at once because he was not pleased with it. These and many other extravagances endeared him to the people and won him a lot of support at election time – candidates could hardly expect to win if they did not entertain at least a few thousand potential voters to sumptuous feasts and to games and gladiatorial spectacles in the arenas of Rome. The extravagances also led the Optimates to believe that Caesar was only a showman, bound to go bankrupt before long, and so they did not worry about the dandified young man with the frilly tunic sleeves. They underrated him completely.

Not long before he set off for Spain, two members of his family who were very close to him died in quick succession. First was his aunt, Julia, the highly respected widow of Marius, who had long been suffering the humiliation of hearing her famous husband's name reviled, even forbidden to be mentioned in polite circles. Caesar used the public speech he was entitled to make at her funeral to regenerate the memory of Marius and to advertise the party which the old man had once led. It was a daring thing to do, but the people rose to the occasion and applauded. They were particularly delighted when he mentioned that his aunt was descended from the old kings of Rome and even from the gods, for the Julii family always claimed Julus, son of Aeneas of Troy and the goddess Venus, as their ancestor.

A few weeks later, his beloved wife Cornelia died. He

mastered his great grief sufficiently to deliver another funeral speech, this time reviving the memory of her father, Cinna, the other great leader of the Populares. The time had come for the Roman people to remember their two champions and to understand that once more their party could become a force in the political scene. His words were not wasted, as he found when he returned from Spain.

With the cheers and clapping of the multitude still ringing in his ears, Caesar set sail for Further Spain. There, he carried out his responsibilities well, it may be presumed because there are no records to the contrary. It was normal for quaestors to make money for themselves in the exercise of their work, and Caesar probably acquired enough to satisfy some, though not all, of his creditors in Rome. He had done so without exciting protests from the provincials who were pleased to promise him a measure of personal support for future days, if he should call for it.

One of the most popular stories about Caesar relates to his time in Spain. It was a legend that grew long after his death, but it has no substance in contemporary history. One day he was visiting Gades (Cadiz) on duty when he noticed a statue of Alexander the Great near the Temple of Hercules. He turned to his friends, with tears in his eyes, and asked to sit down near it. When they enquired why he was weeping, he exclaimed 'Here am I, thirty years old, and I have done nothing worth remembering. At this age he (said Caesar, pointing to Alexander) had conquered the world.' With that, he abruptly ended his term of office in Spain and went back to Rome determined to do some notable act as soon as possible.

Caesar was not that kind of man. The story suggests it was the turning point in his life, but that had already come when he drew Pompey and Crassus together before they stood for the consulship in 71. By then Caesar already knew where he

*The Romans made many kinds of siege engine. This is a model of a 'wild ass',
used for hurling large stones over walls.*

was going and he was content to play his game with patience,
skill, cunning, but in the confidence that things would go his
own way, even if he had to make them. The rest of his career
was an ordered mixture of waiting on events, seizing opportunities, getting people to do what he wanted while letting
them think they were benefitting themselves, negotiating
alliances between the most difficult personalities, organizing
an unparalleled network of informers and agents, many of
whom were women – some even wives of the leading men of
the day, and manipulating the people to give their support to
all manner of projects. While he did this, he continued to
write, to collect art treasures, to spend money – invariably
other people's – to entertain, to advise and to win friends, and
then he went on to become the foremost commander of his
or any age and the greatest statesman the world has seen.
Hardly any of this was by accident. Caesar, of all the great
men of history, made himself what he became.

THREE MEN
RULE ROME

Caesar left Spain in 68. On his way back he sojourned for a while in Cisalpine Gaul, the extremely fertile district in Italy on either side of the river Po. Here, he got to know the leading men of this province. The Gauls north of the Po had not been considered part of Italy after the Social Wars (see page 53) when the Italians were granted Roman citizenship, and now they were beginning to agitate for inclusion. Caesar listened, assessed their strength and gave advice. Probably this was to wait on events, on the understanding that if and when he could help in their demands he would.

He reached Rome to find that nothing had been done to attend to the ills besetting the state. Piracy on the seas was still rampant and food, in the city at all events, was continually short. Mithradates was still unbroken, despite several defeats at the hands of the Optimate general, Lucius Licinius Lucullus. Pompey had retired to his country estate after his consulship and waited in vain for another appointment. Crassus had gone back to his financial empire and was manipulating the business world more or less as he wished. Caesar's own reputation, however, was still high. He had seen to that through his network of agents and publicity men.

Public concern over the pirate menace demanded that something be done. The tribune Aulus Gabinius introduced a bill in the Assembly conferring on Pompey wide powers for dealing with the pirates. These were to include authority to raise men and money anywhere in the empire in the Mediterranean. The command was to last three years. Naturally, the Senate opposed the bill but it was carried. This was an important landmark. A major military command was bestowed not as customary by the Senate but by the will of the people, and it set a precedent of which Caesar had to take advantage in later years.

In a brilliant exercise of efficiency and bold leadership, Pompey rooted out the pirates inside three months, making the seas safe again and enabling the transports to get to and from Rome without interference. This success led to another unorthodox appointment. The Assembly passed a second bill, put forward this time by Caius Manilius, giving Pompey a commission to supersede Lucullus in Asia and finish the war with Mithradates. The measure was hotly debated in the Senate where the majority opposed it, but among those who spoke in its favour were Cicero and Caesar. Flush with his success against the pirates, Pompey set off for the east where in a wonderful campaign he was to cover himself with glory and win for Roman arms their hitherto highest renown.

Pompey's absence was a relief to many. The Senate was glad to do without a popular general who could, as he boasted, at the stamp of his foot marshal an army anywhere in Italy, and perhaps bring it against them. Crassus no longer had to endure listening to the endless huzzahs and paeans of praise which had been uttered everywhere Pompey went in Rome. And for Caesar it presented a splendid interval in which to work on Crassus, undisturbed, to get him to build up his

One of the most authentic portrait busts of Caesar

power and influence so that it would equal that of Pompey. Crassus would need him for this, but Pompey, too, would need him when he came back from the East. What could not the three of them together do for the good of Rome?

In the elections for 65, Caesar stood for the office of curule aedile. There were four of these elected each year. Their duties were concerned with domestic matters such as public games, the police, traffic and roads, markets, public health, and so on. Election gave one a splendid opportunity to make some permanent mark on Rome, to stage some spectacular entertainment, or to introduce some domestic reform that would be remembered. But for this the candidate needed large reserves of money. Again Caesar was woefully overdrawn on his own funds and again he borrowed – heavily – from Crassus. By now he was said to be several millions in debt, but he made no effort to curb his extravagances. One of his first acts as aedile was to stage a vast gladiatorial show, with over three hundred pairs of combatants. This was the biggest programme ever put on, but not content with that he had them all dressed in silver armour. He made himself extremely popular by this and other entertainments. People began to feel that when Caesar put on a show, it would be a professional performance, sensational, magnificent and invariably better than the last.

These shows, the reforming laws with which he was associated, his blunt speeches analysing the country's problems and expressing them in simple terms, certainly made his year as aedile a memorable one. They also made him growingly unpopular with the Optimates who could not fathom what he was aiming at, except that it was obviously not in their interests. When he re-erected in the Forum the memorials and trophies for Marius which had been cast down by Sulla, they became seriously alarmed. He was attacked in the Senate but his answer was that surely it was time to forget the savagery of the old man in his last days and to remember his days as a national hero. But the Optimates, though temporarily baffled by this most reasonable reply, continued to regard him with the greatest suspicion. They were to become more alarmed still during the years to follow.

In 64, an important measure was introduced by the tribune, P. Servilius Rullus, at the instigation of Crassus and Caesar who had worked out the details and who, if it were successful, stood to gain considerable political capital with the Populares. The continuing problem of many thousands of idlers hanging about the streets, waiting for free corn, or looking for trouble of one kind or another was getting more serious. So Rullus proposed that large tracts of land in the district of Campania, and elsewhere in the empire, should be allotted to a substantial proportion of these layabouts. The distribution was to be arranged and supervised by a commission of ten men who were to have the powers of praetors for five years. There were several clauses in the bill dealing with particular land areas in the provinces, which included areas recently conquered by Pompey in his war against Mithradates. The proposals really meant that there would not be anything like enough land left for Pompey to give out to his troops as rewards when the war was concluded. This was intentional, as it provided a check to Pompey's power. The bill was cleverly blocked by Cicero who had been elected one of the consuls for 63, but it made both Crassus and Caesar many new allies without exposing them to attack by the Optimates who may have seen their hands in the measures but could not prove anything.

In 63, Caesar had another important opportunity for advancement but it meant taking considerable risks, for if he lost he would certainly have been ruined forever. Quite apart from anything else, his creditors, probably even Crassus, would have foreclosed and bankrupted him. Characteristically, Caesar seized the chance with boldness, not unmixed with cheek. Quintus Metellus Pius, an Optimate who had been consul in 80 and had been pontifex maximus, or chief priest, of Rome for some years, died. The office which now became vacant was an elective one, and the holder had considerable privileges. To begin with he held it for life. It gave him sole power to decide questions of religious law. This did not bring with it direct political power but it did carry very great political prestige. The office was highly respected.[1] The holder had a splendid house in the Forum, near the Senate House. Perhaps most interestingly, all the previous holders had been elderly men, generally respected, often honourable, men who had given the state a lifetime of service. Even now one of the three candidates for the vacancy was among the most august of the senators, long since retired from active service. He was Publius Servilius Vatia Isauricus, consul in 79, under whom Caesar had been serving as a lieutenant in Asia Minor. The other, hardly less aged but certainly less revered, was Quintus Lutatius Catulus, son of the Catulus who had shared the consulship with Marius in the year of defeat of the Cimbri at Vercellae (101).

To the astonishment of all but his nearest associates and some members of his family, Caesar decided to stand for the vacancy. On the face of it he had everything against him. He was only 36. He was overburdened with debt. He had had numerous liaisons with women, many of them the wives of other men. He had for some time been a serious opponent of the Optimates and had already been accused, though not formally, of plotting to overthrow the state. It is clear that he needed the vacancy very much, for he said to his mother as

[1] It was an office, incidentally, that lasted right into the times when the empire had become Christian, and its name was adopted by the Popes of the Church. It is still the papal title, and Pope Paul VI is still referred to as Pontiff.

he left the house on election day, 'Today you will see me as Chief Priest or you will not see me again', by which he meant that if he lost he would have to go into exile.

But of course he won, and he won handsomely. He had prepared his ground well. Servilius probably did not mind losing too much, but in Catulus, Caesar made a permanent enemy. Catulus had already opposed the two bills giving Pompey the commands against the pirates and Mithridates, and now he joined those other senators who had become convinced that Caesar wanted to overthrow the republic. One of these was Marcus Porcius Cato.

From time to time a nation throws up a man who reaches high office through his abilities but who on the way earns a reputation for integrity and high principles. This reputation for honesty and integrity lasted all Cato's life – and beyond it, but it did not prevent him, when he thought it necessary, from bending rules that he expected other people to obey rigidly. In 59 he approved the spending of money to buy votes in the consular elections to ensure the success of a candidate who would, if elected, be the colleague of Caesar. The candidate, an enemy of Caesar, was M. Calpurnius Bibulus and he was elected.

Born in 95, Cato was the great-grandson of another Marcus Porcius Cato known as Cato the Elder, who in the second century had become famous for his stern and un-yielding character, who devoted much of his later life trying to stop the changes taking place in the Roman character which have been described earlier. For this he was certainly to be admired. But his great-grandson, known as Cato the Younger, even in childhood appears to have affected the same unbending character which his friends mistook for honesty and integrity. He was a quaestor in 65 and in 63 a tribune. He had practised oratory like Caesar and Cicero and was a most forceful speaker. Bearing the same name as his ancestor earned him a respect which his real qualities and character did not merit. Apart from all else he was a heavy drinker whose wits were more often than not fuddled every evening by about dinner time. Having made up his mind about anything, he would never alter it, and he considered anyone who disagreed with him was totally wrong. We do not know when he first developed his intense hatred for Caesar. It may have been when he discovered that his half-sister Servilia, the mother of Brutus (who killed Caesar) had become Caesar's mistress. But by 63 whatever Caesar did or said, Cato would automatically oppose it.

Caesar returned to his house after the election and celebrated his victory with his family whom he told to get ready and pack their things. They were all going to move to the official residence of the Pontifex Maximus, and when they did it was to be Caesar's home for the rest of his life. He does not seem to have developed a taste for the magnificent stately homes on the Palatine Hill that his successors acquired.

The year 63 saw a dangerous threat to the government in Rome. Lucius Sergius Catilina was an impoverished Optimate with an unsavoury past both in office and out of it. When governor of Africa in 67–6 his administration had been so corrupt that he was prosecuted for extortion on his return to Rome. He actually stood for the consulship in 66 but was disqualified. He stood again in 63. He was already desperately short of money. To finance his candidature he had had to borrow more. But as he realized there was a good chance of losing, he had covered himself by planning, with a few disreputable Optimates, to seize power, murder the consuls in office and keep an army in Rome. To get some support from the people for the candidature, he had said he would cancel all debts, but this frightened almost anyone who had money.

Some authorities have said that Crassus and Caesar were involved in his schemes, but this is to misunderstand both men. Crassus did not lend large sums unless he was satisfied that he had a good chance of recovering the loans and the interest. Caesar, as he showed in the Lepidus scheme of 78–7 (page 64) did not lend his support to political programmes which were too extreme or badly planned. Both men actually passed on what they knew about the conspiracy to the consul, Cicero.

The elections came and Catilina was defeated. Immediately, Cicero accused Catilina in the Senate of conspiring to overthrow the republic. He regarded the conspiracy as so dangerous that he persuaded the Senate to issue the ultimate decree. Catilina fled in the hope of joining up with an army in Etruria and bringing it against Rome. Five principal accomplices were arrested on suspicion by Cicero and they were clapped into custody. The Senate was convened to discuss what to do with the captives. A number of senators spoke, mostly urging the death penalty, despite the fact that none of the prisoners had been tried. Then it came to Caesar's turn to speak, and he made a most restrained speech, counselling that the men should not be put to death but should instead be imprisoned for life in large Italian towns, securing them by holding over each town the heaviest possible penalties in case they should escape. At the same time he emphasized the dangers of taking unconstitutional action against the prisoners and in so doing he was covertly warning the Senate not to take the lives of fellow citizens without trial.

Caesar spoke so moderately that it is likely the majority of the Senate would have voted for his proposal. Then Cato spoke, and in no uncertain terms insisted that the death penalty was obligatory, that the prisoners were entitled to no mercy. His hatred of Caesar led him to accuse Caesar of being involved

This very famous picture by Maccari shows Cicero (left) accusing Lucius Sergius Catilina (right) of planning to overthrow the state.

in the conspiracy. He was reaching the climax of his speech when a messenger brought in a letter for Caesar. Caesar opened it, but before he could read it at all, Cato cried out, 'There, you see, he's even had a letter from one of them. He should be made to read it out.'

Caesar glanced at it quickly, then handed it to Cato, inviting him to read it out himself. For a moment or two Cato studied it, then, turning purple with rage, he stalked over to Caesar and flung the paper at him, saying 'Take it, you drunkard!'

This from Cato, of all people, to one who was famous for the moderation with which he drank. The letter was in fact a love letter from Servilia.

Cato's speech won the day and the prisoners were condemned to be put to death at once. An army was sent to deal with Catilina in Etruria, and the unfortunate man was defeated and killed after a very brave fight. Cicero considered that he had saved the state. The Senate, perhaps feeling glad that Cicero had been willing to shoulder the responsibility of putting to death several Optimates without trial, declared Cicero *pater patriae*, 'father of his country', the one among many flattering honours which Cicero quoted time and again in his subsequent speeches in the Senate and in the courts. Still, for a few days he was the hero of Rome, for had he not saved the people from a most terrible danger? This was perhaps an exaggeration, for Catilina's conspiracy could never have succeeded: there were too many things against it.

In the elections of 63, Caesar won one of the eight praetorships. This office was largely judicial, and holders presided over the courts. If the consuls had to leave the city for any reason, praetors took over their work. Praetors were also allotted provinces to govern at the end of their term of office.

The year of Caesar's praetorship was a violent one. It began with trouble. One of the new tribunes, Quintus Metellus

Bust of Pompey, Caesar's friend and rival.

Nepos, had proposed that Pompey should be recalled from the East to restore order in Rome. Caesar supported this. He also gave the Populares a new and unexpected sensation. He proposed that the job of managing the reconstruction of the Temple of Jupiter on the Capitoline Hill should be handed to Pompey. The previous official responsible had been Catulus, and he had had fifteen years to get the work done. Now Caesar demanded that Catulus produce the accounts of his expenditure so far and an explanation of why the temple was not finished. These actions drove the Optimates to consider resort once more to the ultimate decree. Rioting followed. Caesar and Metellus were suspended from their offices. Metellus fled to Pompey in the East. Caesar went home quietly, and from the doorway of his house begged the mob that had followed him not to demonstrate. He closed the door and refused to reappear until he was restored to office.

During the next few days the mob, egged on no doubt by his agents who will have represented his treatment as shameful – which it was, became restive, and crowds began to assemble in huge numbers in the Forum, clamouring for Caesar's reinstatement. The Senate was terrified. Envoys were sent to Caesar's house with an earnest invitation to come back to his office.

During Caesar's year of office Pompey returned from the East, a factor which dominated Roman politics. He was by then unquestionably the greatest man in the world. He had put an end to the power of Mithridates who had committed suicide in 63 rather than fall captive to a Roman general. In his campaign Pompey had conquered vast new areas and brought them under Roman dominion which now stretched to the banks of the river Euphrates. He had overrun Judaea and captured Jerusalem. He had behind him a huge army, rich with booty, anxious to obtain grants of land on which to settle down and make a new life.

When he landed in Italy, everyone asked the same question, what would he do? Would he seize Rome, as Sulla had? The Optimates made overtures to him to get him on their side, but in using Cicero as the principal go-between they wrecked their chances. Cicero, still glowing with self-glorification about his handling of Catilina's conspiracy, had the nerve to compare this relatively minor achievement with Pompey's spectacular success. Pompey's vanity was immediately stirred, and when Caesar, who had anticipated this, came forward with much more realistic ideas, which included immediate recognition of Pompey's pre-eminence in the state, the victorious general was ready to listen. At the same time he made his position clear. He had no wish to be a Sulla. All he wanted was a splendid triumph in the city and grants of land for his men. All Rome was relieved.

Before Caesar's praetorship came to an end, Rome was rocked by a scandal of the greatest sensation. Publius Clodius Pulcher was a young aristocrat who like most younger members of Roman high society played about with revolutionary ideas. He soon discovered, however, that he had formidable powers of working his will upon others, and he decided to make a political career. In Asia Minor he activated a mutiny of Roman troops against their commander, Lucullus, and this was one of the reasons why Pompey was sent out to take over. Clodius was extremely good-looking and made capital of his undoubted attractiveness to women by seducing several well known wives, including, it is believed, Pompeia, the wife of Caesar. Now, in 62, on the eve of being elected quaestor for 61, he conceived a daring adventure.

Towards the end of a year Roman women celebrated the special festival of the Bona Dea, the women's goddess. It was exclusive to women and the rites were held in one or other of the greater houses in the city. This year it was the turn of the Pontifex Maximus to put his house at their disposal. During the celebrations, which were supervised by Caesar's mother, Aurelia, and by Pompeia, Clodius got in disguised as a woman. He wanted to know what happened at the rites. He may also have had an assignation with Pompeia.

Clodius was detected when he let his voice drop to its masculine pitch by accident. Immediately there were screams and giggles, followed by angry rebukes from Aurelia. Clodius was exposed, but before he could be apprehended he fled. A messenger was sent to Caesar to let him know, as head of the Roman religious organization. His response was swift and stern. He proposed to divorce Pompeia. A message was sent to her to tell her to get her things packed and out of his house as soon as convenient. He would stay away until she had left.

The affair began as a foolhardy adventure by an elected official who should certainly have known better. It grew out of all proportion into a political incident. The law had been broken. So the Senate determined to bring Clodius to trial, thinking to discredit Caesar in the process. Clodius' defence was that he was away from Rome on the day concerned and therefore the intruder could not have been he. By careful bribery and some intimidation of the jury he got off. By this time Caesar had left Rome for Spain. Before he set out he had been asked why he divorced Pompeia. 'Because in my judgment members of my household must be as free of suspicion as of crime itself.'

In March, Caesar was allotted the province of Further Spain as governor. He had already been there as quaestor in 69 and was glad to be leaving Rome. His creditors were pressing him hard – and they had much to be pressing about. He probably owed over £2m, and some of them even came down to the harbour at Ostia as he was preparing to embark, threatening to stop the ship and impound his possessions. He sent an urgent letter to Crassus who responded at once with a guarantee of his debts. The ship set sail and for a year Caesar out of the political arena. For him it was an important year. It was his first major command of an army. While he had experience of leading men into battle, he had never organized a whole military campaign, its transports, supplies, arms, administration, or planned its strategy on a broad front. But as in every circumstance where he was faced with a challenge he rose to it and brought to bear all those gifts of his at which Romans were to become increasingly astonished.

Caesar had proved himself an astute politician with an uncanny knack of saying and doing the right things far more often than any of his contemporaries. He was recognized as the organizing genius, if not the head, of the Populares party.

The Optimates, though they hated and feared him, now appreciated that they were dealing with someone of great political and diplomatic skill, not to mention considerable personal charm, who had enormous popular support. He had now to show them he could be a military leader of some consequence.

We know very little about his Spanish command. Evidently he handled the governorship with singular ability. He conquered Lusitania and brought his army right to the shores of the Atlantic Ocean in Galicia. His victorious troops hailed him 'Imperator', a gesture Roman soldiers only made if their commanders really deserved it. He ordered the new territory, leaving it in the hands of Roman and native officials and providing them with an administration with which they were able to run the province efficiently. During his term of office, as was the case with all governors, he accumulated a lot of money. This was raised chiefly by taking a percentage of local taxes and by selling prisoners of war into slavery. While we in the 20th century would regard this as morally wrong, it was perfectly acceptable in first century BC Rome. Where so many governors went wrong amassing great fortunes, earning the hatred of their provincial subjects, and ending up on extortion charges back in the Roman courts, was largely through their greed. They overworked the system. To enlarge the percentages they resorted to terror, cruelty and deceit. And in doing so they did much to damage Rome's reputation throughout the world.

Caesar had seen all this, time and again. He had also taken note of those few governors who had been exceptions, such as Sertorius, happy memories of whom were still nurtured by many. He made enough money to repay the bulk of his debts without hurting the province or its inhabitants. He strengthened the friendships he had made in 69 and built up new ones, and these were to prove valuable later.

Caesar's success had earned him a triumph in Rome. This he would have liked but he wanted the consulship more. Unfortunately, the timing of these events meant that he would have to canvass personally for the consulship and wait outside for a triumph at the same time, which was not allowed. Candidates for the consulship had to canvass inside the city walls. Generals wanting to triumph had to wait outside. Caesar asked the Senate to waive the rules in his case and some were disposed to allowing it. But his enemy Cato deliberately talked against the measure, and did so endlessly until darkness, whereupon the debate had to be adjourned. The measure was not passed. Caesar thereupon gave up the triumph. Those of his supporters who were disappointed because they would not get the fringe benefits of a triumph, feasts, entertainments, hand-outs of money and food, and so on, did not fail to notice how moderate he had been and that Cato and his supporters had shown themselves particularly spiteful.

Caesar's candidature was a landmark in Roman history. He did not merely put himself forward for this highest of elective offices. He made arrangements so that his candidature would be supported – and be seen to be supported – by the two most powerful and influential men in Rome, Pompey and Crassus. To bind these two men to his cause, he seized upon their most outstanding grievances against the Optimates in the Senate. In Pompey's case, the Senate, with typical ingratitude, refused to ratify his arrangements in the East and they opposed the land settlements for his troops. As for Crassus, he had wanted a revision of the revenue collecting system in Asia, not only for himself but for the tax collectors as a class. Tax collecting had been farmed out to a company of gatherers – called publicani – and the contract was not bringing them good enough returns. The Senate had refused to alter the contract.

By very careful negotiation, for Crassus and Pompey still distrusted one another, Caesar got them to back his candidature, on the understanding that he would, if elected, legislate for their requirements. In return he wanted an important military command when his term of office was over. The support was promised and he was easily elected for 59. His colleague for the year was Marcus Calpurnius Bibulus, the Optimate friend of Cato, who was supported with vast sums of money for bribing the electorate by the Optimates in the hope that he would, if elected, frustrate every move Caesar made. They were right in thinking he would obstruct Caesar. On practically every measure brought in by Caesar, Bibulus announced that the omens were unfavourable and that therefore the Senate could not discuss it.

Caesar's consulship was packed with excitement. A few days before the election the Optimates had got the Senate to agree that whoever became consul in 59 should at the end of their year be commissioned to look after the forests and woodland paths of Italy. This insulting commission was aimed at Caesar, to make him powerless in the year after his consulship (if he were elected), in which case they could undo any acts he might get through during his year. Almost from the moment he was elected he was obstructed by Bibulus, Cato, Catulus and their henchmen. This unhelpful attitude resulted in the coming together of Caesar, Pompey and Crassus in a three-party agreement to rule Rome. They promised each other not to take any political step without the full knowledge and approval of each other. Later ages were to call the arrangement the rule by the Triumvirate. As long as they remained in agreement they were unassailable, and it was through Caesar's matchless skill as a diplomatist that the Triumvirate lasted several years, when it had everything against it. To fortify the alliance, Pompey who had divorced his wife Mucia in 62, now married Caesar's only daughter Julia, beautiful, talented, unmarried, and the apple of her father's eye. Caesar himself married again and his new wife was Calpurnia, daughter of Lucius Calpurnius Piso, who was to be a candidate for consul in 58.

One of Caesar's first acts as consul was to introduce the Acta Diurna, a daily report of proceedings in the Senate and in the Assembly. This was posted in the Forum, and probably at other centres of activity, for all to read. It was the first public newsheet in the world and is sometimes cited by communications historians as the origin of newspapers. Another act was to bring forward an agrarian law to distribute land for about 20,000 settlers, including Pompey's troops, in Campania. A third was to ratify Pompey's eastern arrangements and a fourth was to revise the Asian tax contract. A fifth, the Julian law against extortion in the provinces had far-reaching results. It remained in force for hundreds of years, up to the collapse of the Western Roman Empire in the late fifth century AD, and it cracked down upon extortion so hard that before long oppressive and grasping governors were a very rare exception and not, as they had been, the rule.[1]

These important laws were not carried without considerable trouble. Caesar began by trying politeness; the proposals were outlined and comment was invited. Nothing came of this; the Optimates would not even consider them; they merely stone-walled. So Caesar said he would take it to the Assembly where he knew he would get a majority in favour. His colleague Bibulus vetoed this and retired again to study the omens. Caesar's patience was beginning to run out. He discussed the matter with Pompey and Crassus, and they made a plan. They called upon the services of one of the tribunes,

---

[1] In later years, when he was master of the world, Caesar picked as governors men noted for ability and honesty, and not for family influence.

A Roman wall painting of the harbour at Puteoli, near Naples. It was at a jetty like the one in the centre that Caesar was stopped by creditors when he was about to set sail for Spain from Ostia

Publius Vatinius, a loyal and courageous ally who was said to be the ugliest man in Rome. Vatinius proposed in the Assembly that Caesar should be given Cisalpine Gaul and Illyricum as his proconsular province when his term of office ended, and that he should have it for five years. Pompey, whose vanity did not allow him even to consider that Caesar might prove a better general, did not think it dangerous to give him an army north of the Italian border.

The Optimates persuaded three other tribunes to block the bill, but by this time the Triumvirate – and the people – had had enough. The measure was put to the Assembly direct and it was carried by a large majority. To discourage further Optimate opposition, Pompey had summoned a number of his troops, in civilian clothing, to the Forum. They filled the area outside the Assembly. There, Caesar called to Pompey 'And if, after the electors have passed our bills, our enemies resort to the sword—?'. Pompey answered 'Then I will resort to sword and buckler, too' and clapped a gloved hand to the pommel of his sword.

Bibulus now retired permanently to his house announcing that he would stay there to study the omens indefinitely. Constitutionally, this meant that no state business could be conducted. But Caesar had become indifferent to such outdated conceptions and he completed his whole programme with the support of the Assembly. Many people, instead of referring to the year, as was the custom, by the names of the two consuls in office, began to call it 'In the consulship of Julius and Caesar.'

He had succeeded in doing what the Gracchi brothers had given their lives for. The Assembly was once again, as it had been of old, supreme over the Senate.

Pompey, meanwhile, proposed in the Senate that Caesar's command should be extended to include Transalpine Gaul, and the Senate approved. Perhaps many of his enemies hoped that Caesar would perish there among the barbarous trouser-wearing Celts.

For Caesar the prospect of commanding a number of legions for five years in Gaul was one filled with excitement and challenge. Beyond the Alps was a huge and unconquered territory, and in it possibly enormous wealth and certainly unparalleled military prestige were there to be won. He was already superior to Pompey and Crassus in political skill and diplomacy, but he had been quite content to take second place under their shadow. But if he could win a new empire and acquire the kind of wealth Crassus had made, would this not give him the power to reconstruct the tottering and decaying republic? Pompey had the power but not the capability; Crassus probably had the ability but he did not have the interest. Caesar can hardly be criticized if, realizing that he was the only person who could tackle this necessary job, he began preparations for the bid for absolute power that the circumstances demanded. Why it should have been necessary to spend nearly ten years in Gaul to get ready for this moment will become clear in the next chapter.

CISALPINE GAUL

R. Po
Ravenna
R. Rubicon
Luca
Ancona
Auximum
Pisa
Asculum
R. Tiber
Rome
ITALY
Ostia
Capua
Cannae
(216 B.C.)
Brundisium
Tarentum

ADRIATIC SEA

Lissus
Dyrrachium
MACEDONIA
GREECE

Pharsalus
(48 B.C.)

Messina

Lilybaeum
Corinth
Athens

SICILY

MEDITERRANEAN SEA

200 m
320 km

N

VI

GAUL AND BRITAIN

Caesar's consulship ended almost as dramatically as it had begun. Hardly had the new officials for 58 taken office when two praetors, Lucius Domitius Ahenobarbus (Redhead) and Caius Memmius, demanded a senatorial enquiry into his acts. The Senate began to discuss the subject but when Ahenobarbus proposed that the acts be annulled, a tribune, probably Clodius, vetoed it, and the whole business was dropped. Caesar had by that time left Rome for Gaul, and so could not be tried in his absence in any case. He had left the management of his party and the cause of reform in the hands of Clodius whose gangs of political demonstrators, rabble-rousers and bullies dominated the streets of Rome. The presence of Pompey and Crassus would restrain the gangs from too many excesses, he hoped, and keep a moderating hand on Clodius himself.

Two leading opponents, Cato and Cicero, were swiftly neutralized. Cato was appointed head of a commission to annexe the kingdom of Cyprus, a job likely to take at least two years. Cicero, whom Caesar had invited to join the Triumvirate and make a Committee of Four but who had refused, now paid for his unwillingness to cooperate. Clodius moved a bill re-stating the law that anyone who put to death a Roman citizen without trial should himself be driven into exile. He made it retrospective, which implicated Cicero who had executed the five supporters of Catilina in 63 (page *88*). Before the bill could be passed, Cicero left the city. Caesar could now feel that for the next few years he would be safe and that whatever fortune befell him in Gaul his position at Rome would not be undermined.

At 41, Caesar was among the best-looking men in Rome. His handsomeness was if anything enhanced by a baldness which, however, worried him a great deal and which he tried to conceal by combing what hair he had forwards over the top of his head. Portrait bust sculptors have captured this feature well (see page *23*). He was one of the most prominent men in social, as well as political, life. His affairs with women were notorious in his own time but may well have been exaggerated by later historians. The longest lasting and probably the deepest felt was his love affair with Servilia (page *88*) which he advertized by giving her the most expensive presents. One, a pearl, was said to have cost 60,000 gold pieces (£60,000), for which no doubt he borrowed the money from Crassus.

Caesar had wonderful charm and perfect manners. People who met him remembered him for the way he always put them at their ease and made them the centre of attention when he spoke to them. He never took too much to drink which led Cato to remark that he was the only sober man to try to wreck the Constitution.[1] No one could ever take exception to his behaviour, except once or twice in his last years and this may well have been because he was in the throes of an attack of

---

[1] Among others who tried to wreck the Constitution in Roman history, Marius, Sulla, and Catilina, were notoriously heavy drinkers: so was Cato himself.

epilepsy (see page *168*). On one occasion he was at a dinner where the host's waiters served rancid oil by mistake. The other guests coughed and spluttered and some even asked for their plates to be taken away. Caesar, to spare his host from further embarrassment, helped himself more liberally to the oil and took it down with relish. As a conversationalist Caesar was not witty like Cicero or the poet Catullus, though he had a strong sense of humour. But he was profoundly learned and could talk on almost any subject with knowledge, and always with a readiness to listen to other people's views.

This remarkable personality was now about to demonstrate an amazing capacity for leading men in prolonged warfare and of sharing to the full their hardships, a quality his contemporaries did not realize he had, and of which he himself may not have been aware.

Caesar's Gallic War has been immortalized by his Commentaries on them. There can be few schoolboys who have not had to try to translate the opening paragraphs of the first book, beginning 'Gallia est omnis divisa in partes tres' – 'All Gaul is divided into three parts', and have cursed or champed at what seemed hard work. But in comparison with other Latin authors, Caesar's style was pure, compact, lucid, 'made up of words that are simple and unerringly chosen' (Professor Grant). The work, consisting of seven books which he wrote and one written by his officer, Aulus Hirtius, has become one of the great works of history. It was the simple, albeit one-sided, account by a man of action of his actions in the course of a long series of campaigns, and it is the only such surviving account written by a general in command. It was regarded as a masterpiece of military history by, among others, Napoleon and Wellington, both of whom recommended it to students of war.

The great value of the Commentaries is that they give an

authentic picture of Caesar: so did his later Commentaries on the Civil War. Much of what is known about him up to his setting out for Gaul and in the last two years or so of his life comes from historians of one political persuasion or another writing after his time, though they will have been able to read contemporary letters, documents, descriptions and accounts not available to us. His books were intended to be propaganda, to justify his conduct of the war which was from time to time to be questioned in the Senate. Each book of the Gallic War covers about a year and the whole lot were probably published at the end of 51 BC.

Gaul as Caesar was to know it included France, Belgium and parts of Switzerland, Holland and Germany, with that stretch of Italy from the Apennine mountains to the Alps. The Romans already occupied the stretch to the Alps. Beyond that the Gaul that was independent (Free Gaul) consisted of three principal nations, groups of tribes who were very loosely knit. These were the Belgae who occupied the north-west area, the Aquitani the south-west, and the Celtae the remainder. Well over ten million, perhaps as many as fifteen million, people lived here. They were on the whole civilized by Roman standards though there were some differences. Perhaps the most serious was their poor system of government. The Gallic mania for fighting amongst themselves made any form of practical central government impossible. The tribes elected their chiefs and threw them over in favour of new ones with alarming frequency. If a chief built up any sort of dominion, it was doomed not to last. No chief could depend upon the word of an ally in times of emergency.

On the other side of the coin, Caesar found the Gauls fascinating. True, they believed in human sacrifice and were not troubled by such conceptions as justice. But they were gifted artists and poets, potters and weavers, sculptors and ironsmiths. They knew how to build fortifications. They had constructed towns, bridges and roads. On the Atlantic coast they were skilled shipbuilders and sailors. They made skiffs of leather and wood, with wooden oars for short distances, and they made larger vessels of oak, with flat bottoms, high bows and sterns, with sails, which were quite capable of riding the

Three swords used by the Gauls in Caesar's campaign. Their favourite was the long two-edged sword which they wielded with great strength and enthusiasm.

great rolling waves of the Atlantic.

The Gauls were extremely warlike. Their best artwork is invariably found as decorations on shields, helmets and other accoutrements of battle. But they were quite unable to accept the type of discipline to which a Roman army was accustomed, and in battle, once the initial shock of confrontation had passed, they often broke up into individual fighting units. As such they were easy prey to the more ordered Roman legions.

While he was preparing to set out for his province, Caesar had been well briefed by agents as to what was going on among the various tribes in Gaul and its neighbours. The

Helvetii, a tribe of some 350,000 people which occupied what is now Switzerland, were threatening to move into Gaul across the river Rhône. There were two routes; one, a narrow and tortuous path between the Jura mountains and the river, through the land of the Sequani, and the other, a much easier road, across the bridge at Geneva into Transalpine Gaul

This is a Roman coin showing the head of a Gaul. It has been suggested that the head is of Vercingetorix.

through the area occupied by the Allobroges. They elected to take the easier road even though it meant risking an open confrontation with Rome.

As soon as he heard, Caesar left Rome and rode with astonishing swiftness to Geneva which he reached inside eight days, riding about 90 miles a day. When he arrived no one was expecting him, least of all the Helvetii. He ordered the general mobilization of troops in the area and instructed his engineers to destroy the bridge. When the Helvetii heard of this they sent a delegation to protest. Caesar, having discovered that about 100,000 of them were fit to bear arms, decided to play for time so that he could marshal the remainder of his legions and their equipment. He told the delegates he would consider their protests and give them an answer in two weeks. In the interval, he constructed a line of earthwork fortifications about 18 miles long between Geneva and the mountains, in case the Helvetii should try to cross the river. They did try but were beaten back. So they attempted the more difficult route.

Caesar regarded this as dangerous and he determined to stop it. He appointed as second in command an old colleague of his political days, Titus Labienus, who had been tribune in 63, and left him in charge while he dashed back to Italy to collect the rest of his forces. When he was given command in Gaul he had been allotted four legions, the 7th, 8th, 9th and 10th, and now he recruited two more. Then, by a series of forced marches he returned to Switzerland via the Alps and came up behind the Helvetii, while they were in the act of crossing the river Sãone. He routed a section of their army which had not crossed, and then moved away. The rest of the Helvetii thought he was retiring – which is what he wanted them to do – and they pursued him. Not far from Bibracte Caesar positioned his legions in three lines on the slope of a hill, with his reserves on the hillcrest.

The Helvetii charged into the battle area, expecting to roll back the Romans through sheer superiority of numbers. But they were met with a terrifying hail of weapons, chiefly well-aimed javelins, which threw their forward ranks into disorder. Quick to exploit this, Caesar ordered the first two lines to advance and in no time at all the Helvetii were being chased across the fields. Some rallied a little further off and attacked Caesar's right wing, but Caesar sent the third line into this force and broke it up. The news spread through the rest of the Helvetians and their army disintegrated. As they ran from the

A model of a section of the fortifications Caesar put up outside Alesia in 52 BC.

field they were cut down in hundreds. The survivors surrendered and were sent home back into their own lands.

The news of Caesar's first victory was received with joy by many of the Gallic tribes, and in Rome with some amazement that he should be capable of the astute generalship people generally associated only with Pompey. But there was much more to come.

While the Gauls were congratulating Caesar, they also drew his attention to another danger on the borders, from Ariovistus, king of the Suebi tribe from Germany, who in 59 BC had been dubbed 'Friend of the Roman People' by the Senate. This savage chief was threatening to invade Gaul again. He had already bullied the Sequani and the Aedui and seized large and prosperous farmland areas of their territories. Caesar decided to call a meeting to discuss these problems, but when he sent a message to Ariovistus, the German merely answered: 'If I want anything of Caesar, I will go to him: if he wants anything of me, he can come to me.'

Caesar replied by sending Ariovistus another note requesting him not to bring any more troops across the Rhine into Gaul, and to stop provoking the Aedui and Sequani. Ariovistus dared Caesar to go to war, and at once began to march towards Vesontio (Besançon). Caesar anticipated this by one of his night-and-day forced marches and arrived there first.

Suddenly, he was faced with a mutiny in his army. Some of the junior officers, mainly young men of patrician birth who had come out with Caesar for adventure, became demoralized by the reports they heard of the huge and terrifying appearance of the Germans. In no time, they had spread alarm through the ranks, even among hardened centurions. Caesar reacted at once; he was always at his best at moments of crisis. He summoned officers and centurions to a meeting and addressed them sharply. What business of

In the front a Gaul wields a long two-edged sword at a Roman legionary. At right is a Gallic cottage of wooden walls and thatched roof.

theirs was it to ask where he was leading them or to spread stories about what the Germans were like? He proposed to strike camp earlier than originally planned and would advance against the enemy before sunrise. If they did not wish to come with him, they could go back to Rome. He would go it alone with the 10th Legion, on whom he knew he could count. This had the desired effect. The 10th were delighted by being singled out. The others vied with each other to win their commander's favour. And when it came, the battle was swift and decisive. The Germans were cut to pieces where they stood. Those that fled from the field were hunted down by the cavalry and slain. Among them were two wives of Ariovistus. The king fled across the river and died soon afterwards. There was no more trouble from that part of Germany for many years.

After these two successes, which were received with some indifference in Rome, Caesar withdrew into winter quarters, for armies in those times did not usually engage in warfare in winter months. He left Labienus in charge and rode off to Cisalpine Gaul. There he spent some time considering his next move. He had grasped well the essential weakness of the Gauls, divided as they were into a hundred jealous tribes, and he saw that they wanted, even if they did not actually say so, unification under a strong central administration. Clearly no tribe was going to acknowledge another as superior, though for a short while in 52 most of Gaul was united under Vercin-getorix, chief of the Arverni (page *123*). Here was a great opportunity for Rome to extend its civilization and empire. Here was a people, hopelessly divided but who would not only benefit from Roman government but also would in turn con-tribute enormously to the empire. So he planned the conquest of Gaul, and he would achieve it with any army of at first eight and later of ten legions. How was this army constituted?

A first century AD cavalryman, possibly from the Second Legion stationed in Britain, in Gloucestershire.

The military reforms of Marius in the last years of the previous century had put the army on a professional basis. It was no longer necessary to be a property owner to serve. Anyone who was a Roman citizen – and in Caesar's time this included Italians – could enlist and receive pay in the legions. The formation of the army had changed, too. On paper a legion was divided into ten cohorts, and every cohort (except the most senior one) has six centuries of 80 men each, making 480. The most senior cohort had 800 men. Each legion also had 128 light cavalry attached to its strength. This gave a strength of over 5200, but in practice throughout Caesar's campaigns the legion's number were more like 4000 men and 100 cavalry.

The centuries were the backbone of the army. Each was commanded by a centurion, assisted by an optio. The cohort of which the centuries were part was commanded by a senior centurion. In Caesar's army each centurion was picked on the strength of his high reputation for fearlessness, toughness and skill. Caesar seems to have been particularly devoted to them, as they are mentioned often in his books. Perhaps his favourite was Gaius Crastinus who died (for him) in the civil war (page *143*).

The legionary was a foot-soldier, who wore thick-soled sandals or hob-nailed shoes. He was dressed in iron or hardened leather armour under which he wore a sleeveless woollen tunic. He wore a bronze crested helmet, carried a dished oval shield, and was armed with a short sword which was equally effective for thrusting as for cutting. He also carried a variety of spears, including the pilum, a heavy throwing javelin, about 7 ft long. This had a long thin iron which continued into the wooden shaft for some distance. It could penetrate armour or encumber an opponent's shield very effectively. Lighter and shorter spears could be thrown for great distances, well over 100 ft.

While on the march legionaries carried everything they needed on their backs, armour, stakes for trenches, saws, baskets, spades, axes, cooking pots, a supply of corn, as well as javelins and their shield. The combined weight of these was over 45 lbs. The heavier baggage like tents, mechanical weapons, and so forth, were carried on wagons or by baggage animals.

Each legion carried various standards or emblems for identification and as marks of honour. The most important was the legion's aquila, or eagle, of gold on silver bolts, carried by a standard bearer marching with the senior cohort. Legionaries followed the glistening emblem which was raised high and

How a 14th Century artist saw the invasion of Britain by Caesar. Most of the detail is wrong: chain mail, bows and arrows, and heraldic banners were not features of Caesar's armies

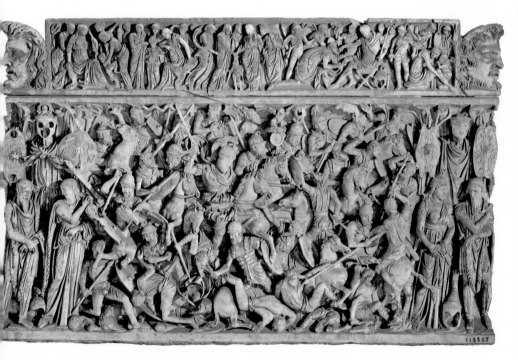

Sarcophagus depicting a battle scene. The Romans are fighting a barbarian army

they were spurred on to deeds of valour by the urge to protect it, for it was regarded as an appalling disgrace to lose it to the enemy.

The legions were commanded by a general who wore a scarlet cloak of wool embroidered with gold. He had under him a number of legates, usually men selected from the senatorial membership. Few of these were ever allowed any independence of action; the success or failure of a Roman army depended largely upon the leadership of its general.

In addition to the infantry legions and the light cavalry, there were detachments of non-Roman cavalry assisting them, and the riders were mostly from Gaul, Spain or Germany. In Caesar's army these might run into several hundreds. He used them to pursue fleeing enemy forces. There were also other assisting forces (or auxiliaries), lightly armed men, also foreign, such as archers from Crete, stone slingers from the Balaeric Islands, and javelin throwers from Numidia in North Africa. These men were commanded by Roman officers.

Another body attached to the legion was the corps of engineers, blacksmiths, carpenters and so on who repaired armour, kept the siege engines working, designed and laid out the fortifications, bridges and towers needed by an army.

Stringing along behind a Roman army was a rag-bag assortment of hangers-on, slaves acting as valets to the troops, sutlers who sold provisions, merchants who bought items of booty and paid in cash, traders of all kinds who brought their stalls with them, and sometimes camp followers for the men's delights after battle.

These were the ingredients of Caesar's army in Gaul which was now poised for a major campaign.

Caesar returned to Gaul in the spring of 57, refreshed by a winter in northern Italy, satisfied that his agents had his interests in Rome securely under control. He now had eight legions of nearly 40,000 men, and with these he marched against the Belgae who were massing against him in northern France. He crushed the first two tribes, the Suessiones and the Bellovaci, and then he came upon the land of the Nervii, a particularly ferocious tribe of great numbers who lived in the flat wooded countryside above the river Sambre in what is to-day Belgium, the land where in later centuries some of the most famous battles in history were fought.[1] Here, Caesar's army was momentarily surprised by these bold warriors, the toughest he had so far encountered. For some while a battle raged. On the right of the Roman lines a huge Nervian force crashed into the 12th Legion and in minutes killed many centurions. Caesar saw this from his observation platform, rushed down to the thick of the fray, snatched a shield from a soldier and charged forwards shouting to his men – 'Hey! You! Follow me!', calling them by their names. He always knew the names of his officers and centurions – and of a good many ordinary legionaries, too – a wonderful way in which to build up a close bond between commander and commanded.

This did not end the battle but it saved the day. Then, faithful Labienus appeared near the river with two more legions and before sunset the Nervii were surrounded. They chose not to yield but to fight to the death. 50,000 of them perished where they stood. Only the elderly leaders who had kept out of the battle survived and yielded. It was a memorable victory, '. . . that day he o'ercame the Nervii' as Shakespeare's Mark Antony reminded the angry populace in Rome when he addressed them after Caesar's murder in 44 BC. It created a sensation when the news reached Rome. The Senate pro-

---

[1] Crecy, 1346; Agincourt, 1415; Waterloo, 1815.

claimed a public holiday of thanksgiving, called a supplicatio, for fifteen days, the longest ever decreed. Pompey's victory over Mithradates had only earned ten.

Soon afterwards Caesar returned to winter quarters again in Cisalpine Gaul where he had discussions over several weeks with agents who came to visit him from Rome. There, he learned that Cicero had returned from exile to a great welcome. He had been one of the main movers of a Senate proposal that Pompey should be given a new five year commission, to manage the supply of grain to the city whose organization had broken down. It was not much but it was all the Senate dared offer him in a subtle attempt to detach him from Caesar. Clodius, meanwhile, had begun to make himself very unpopular with his violent street gangs who were sent out to organize rioting at every opportunity. Pompey retaliated by hiring an equally violent demagogue, Titus Annius Milo, whose gangs could any time equal those of Clodius.

By the beginning of 56 BC Caesar had become seriously disturbed by developments. The Senate was more openly trying to detach Pompey. It had recovered enough courage to press for an enquiry into Caesar's agrarian law of 59 which had settled land on Pompey's troops in Campania. Ahenobarbus, now a candidate for the 55 consulship, made clear his intention to demand Caesar's recall. Pompey himself was thoroughly riled by the Clodian gangs. It was time to take action to strengthen the Triumvirate, and here Caesar's unique negotiating skill enabled him to convince both Crassus and Pompey that their interests – and those of Rome – were better served if the Committee hung together. Caesar held a conference with Crassus at Ravenna, on the border of Roman Italy (for no proconsul was allowed to enter Italy during his term of command) and a short while afterwards one with Pompey and Crassus at Luca. There, no less than 200 senators assembled, enough to form a constitutional senatorial meeting whose decisions could be binding on the Senate at Rome.

It was a momentous conference. The Triumvirate was renewed. Crassus and Pompey were to have the consulship for 55, and then to have Syria and Spain, respectively, as their proconsular provinces for five years thereafter. Caesar's command in Gaul was to be extended by five more years, that is, up to 49 BC. In that year he was to stand for the consulship again. For Crassus the arrangement was particularly welcome; he had long wanted another big military command and here was an opportunity to lead Roman arms against the kingdom of Parthia. Pompey cannot have been so pleased, though his command was in addition to his already wide powers as director of corn supplies, and he was allowed to administer his province through delegated officials. Therein, perhaps, lay one of the causes of his ultimate destruction. Had he actually governed Spain himself, he might have won enough allies there to stand behind him in his eventual confrontation with Caesar in 49 and 48. Another good thing came out of this conference. Cicero was invited to join the committee. He did not accept but he did indicate that he would speak in favour of the arrangements in the Senate. In particular, he praised Caesar's achievements in Gaul. He had good reason to do so. Of all his contemporaries, only Caesar had always been kind and helpful. Whatever Caesar thought about Cicero's attitudes in the past, he never let this interfere with their friendship. While he was undoubtedly behind Clodius' move to get Cicero exiled, he never allowed Cicero to know it. Cicero, though high-minded and well-meaning, was a serious obstacle to improving the political situation in Rome at the time. Now, Cicero wrote to his friend Atticus 'I shall see that those who have been kind to me shall have my support'. His brother Quintus joined Caesar's staff as a commander and performed many deeds of heroism.

The Luca conference gave Caesar the time to consolidate his grip on Gaul and to enhance his reputation. It frustrated the schemes of Ahenobarbus who was no longer able to interfere. It pacified Caesar's two colleagues in the Committee of Three. But it was also the last time the three men met; Crassus never saw Caesar again and Pompey was only seen by Caesar from a distance at the battle of Pharsalus in 48.

Caesar needed the extra time. In 56 he had to face the first revolts against Roman authority, among the tribes of Western Gaul, the Aquitani in the south-west and the Veneti in what is now Brittany. In Aquitania he sent Public Licinius Crassus, old Crassus' son who had already proved a splendid field commander, and against the Veneti he sent Decimus Junius Brutus, another able commander who over the next few years was to receive many favours from Caesar and in 44 was to be one of his murderers.

Brutus' engagement with the Veneti was the first sea battle ever fought in the Atlantic by a Roman fleet. The Veneti had by far the largest fleet of ships of the coastal tribes of Gaul. They were well versed in navigation and their whole lives were given to the sea, to ship-building and maritime trading. Their flat-bottomed ships, with high bows and sterns, were built stoutly of oak timbers at least a foot thick held together with huge iron nails. Their anchor cables were iron chains. Their sails were of leather for the canvas or sail cloth of those days was not strong enough to stand up to Atlantic winds.

To deal with this fleet, Caesar had his own ships built on the conventional Roman pattern, galleys with oars and mounted with turrets. These lighter vessels were faster. Caesar had also studied the construction of the Venetian ships, and he ordered his shipwrights to make hundreds of long poles with pointed hooks at the ends. When the enemy assembled their ships, a vast armada of over 200 vessels, and began to bear down upon the smaller Roman craft, Brutus, who was in command, ordered his ships at high speed into the Venetian lines. The ships got close to the bigger Gallic craft, the Romans lifted up their poles, hooked them round the halyards of the Venetian sails, and pulled. And as they did the steersmen turned the ships about and made off, tightening the enemy sail ropes until they snapped. In no time the bulk of the Venetian ships were rendered useless. They could not sail and the crews were submerged beneath masses of heavy wet sails. Their capture or destruction was easy.

As Caesar himself noted, 'After that it was a soldier's battle, in which the Romans easily proved superior.' In a battle lasting from about ten in the morning to sunset, the Romans triumphed, and the revolt was over. It had been a revolt, a breach of faith, and Caesar decided to punish the Venetians, as a lesson to others. The leading men were executed; the remainder were sold into slavery.

The first and among the most memorable dates the British learn of their own history is 55 BC, the year when Caesar crossed the channel and invaded Kent. The year was hardly less sensational for the Romans. An enormous German army was destroyed and a huge bridge was built across the Rhine in under a fortnight, by any standards an amazing engineering feat.

Two powerful German tribes, the Usipetes and the Tencteri, had crossed the Rhine into Gaul in search of living space, It was soon clear to Caesar that they were looking for trouble, for they began stirring up certain discontented Gallic leaders. Caesar ordered them to leave Gaul. When their leaders came to discuss the matter with him, some of their followers attacked a detachment of Roman cavalry. This was treachery. Caesar detained the leaders and ordered his men to attack their armies. A terrible carnage followed and nearly all the Germans were slain, with practically no loss on the Roman side. Those who were not killed on the field were drowned in the fast current of the river. This was not the first time a Germanic tribe had acted with such treachery, and Caesar had thought it right to make an example of them. It was, however, un-characteristically harsh and perhaps he deserved the criticism he got for it in the Senate.

Caesar was now determined to show the German peoples that the Romans were perfectly capable of fighting them on their own ground, too. At a point somewhere near Coblenz, he decided to build a bridge and take an army across into their land. The river was wide and deep. The materials were still standing as trees in a wood nearby. And yet in ten days a com-plete bridge with a forty foot wide road was constructed on well-based piles, so placed, as Caesar himself said 'that the greater the force of the current the more tightly were the piles held in position.'

Immediately the bridge was completed, Caesar took a legion across it, marched into German territory, and rounded up the straggling remnants of the tribes. Then he returned to Gaul, destroying the bridge behind him. Scouts had told him that the undertaking had had its effect; the Germans were terrified.

Caesar then moved on to Normandy, where he assembled an invasion fleet and made plans to sail across the channel to the hitherto little known islands of Britain. There, the British Celts had been giving refuge to disaffected Gauls and encour-aging them to rebel against Roman rule. Presumably they had also been supplying them with fresh arms and provisions. This was enough for Caesar. An added incentive was the prospect of exploring an entirely new land where he had heard fresh pearls abounded. And of course an invasion would give his agents in Rome splendid material for a new publicity campaign on his behalf. He had not been seen for over three years by the people.

On 26th August he set sail with about eighty ships carrying two legions from somewhere between Calais and Boulogne and by about 10.00 am the next morning he reached somewhere near Romney. There on the shore he saw a British contingent of horsemen and some chariots. He leapt down from his ship and led his men ashore. A quick battle followed and the British were driven off. Caesar built a camp a mile or so from the beach and prepared to explore further inland. Almost at once the British asked for peace. While he was arranging the terms a storm blew up and damaged many of his transports, delaying his return to Gaul.

It had only been a brief exploration and nothing of value had been achieved. Yet when his despatches were read by the Senate in Rome they decreed a supplicatio of twenty days. Caesar was greatly encouraged and planned to return to Britain, this time, he hoped, to conquer the British and bring them into the empire. All winter he had special transport ships built, probably several hundred of them, for when he was ready to embark in July 54 he had over 800 ships. On the 20th, a week after his 46th birthday, with five legions and 2000 cavalrymen with their horses packed beneath the decks, Caesar set sail and landed in the area of Sandwich. Immediately he pitched camp and set out for the interior. This time he reached somewhere near Canterbury. There, an army of Celts was drawn up to meet him. On the sides of the main body of infantry were their formidable chariots. The Celtic troops had tried to make themselves more frightening by painting woad, a blue dye, all over their faces and limbs. But Caesar was an old hand at the terror game and his men were now quite used to facing any risks he asked of them.

The British were driven off the field and retreated north of the Thames to St. Albans (in Latin, Verulamium) where their king, Cassivellaunus, held court. Caesar pursued them, crossing the Thames somewhere between Walton and Sunbury, and at Wheathampstead, near Hertford, he defeated them again. Cassivellaunus sued for peace. Caesar took hostages and imposed a heavy tribute (or fine) which they did not pay. It was too complex a task to conquer the whole island – indeed he cannot have been very sure how large or what shape it was. He had also received some disturbing news from Labienus whom he had left in Gaul. So he headed back at once.

Labienus reported that there was serious trouble building up among the conquered Gauls. So far, there was no sign of unity, but some of the tribes were independently plotting revolt. Caesar therefore re-positioned his legions in order to be able to contain rebellion wherever it might break out. But no one can be everywhere at once, and when it did begin it was in an unexpected manner. One of the legions had been posted to the district around Liege. It consisted largely of recruits from Gaul who appeared to be loyal to Rome. They were commanded by two Roman officers, Quintus Titurius Sabinus and Lucius Aurunculeius Cotta (who may have been a relative of Caesar). The chief of the tribe concerned, the Eburones, was called Ambiorix, and he led his men against the Romans only to be beaten off. Then he asked for discussions. He told Sabinus and Cotta that a dangerous revolt was about to erupt not far from where Caesar was, about 100 miles away, and that he thought they should go and join him. Cotta disbelieved Ambiorix and declined to move out of the camp until he heard directly from Caesar. Sabinus accepted Ambiorix' story and persuaded the legion to march out. And so they did – right into an ambush. Cotta was slain fighting to the end; Sabinus survived to beg for mercy from Ambiorix –

and he was rewarded by being cut down.

Ambiorix now fancied himself leader of a great Gallic con-
federation, and he talked the Nervii into attacking another
Roman legion's encampment at Charleroi, under Cicero's
brother Quintus. Quintus sent messengers to Caesar asking
for reinforcements and assuring his chief that till they came
he would fight to the last where he stood. And so it nearly
happened, for the first messengers never got through. They
were caught and put to death. Then one did reach Caesar who
replied at once that he would come to the rescue. He sent his
reply in Greek so that the Gauls would not understand it if this
messenger was caught. By night the messenger reached
Quintus's camp and hurled a spear over the battlements.
Attached to it was the message. Not far behind came Caesar's
forces and Quintus was relieved.

Caesar was greatly impressed at the gallant fight Quintus
and his men had put up. He ordered a parade of the legion
and found that not one in ten of the legionaries were un-
wounded. He congratulated them all, singling out centurions
and tribunes for special mention, and then in front of everyone
he showered praise upon Cicero.

For the next year, his campaigns continued to be directed
against sporadic rebellions in one part of Gaul or another.
This was worrying enough, but far more disturbing news
began to tumble in from Rome.

In 54, Caesar's mother Aurelia died, content at least to have
lived to see her son become a great general. Then his daughter
Julia died in childbirth, and her son – Pompey's son, too – did
not survive many days. Both deaths affected Caesar deeply,
but Julia's had the saddest political results. It broke up the
Triumvirate. The bond between him and Pompey had gone.
In 53, more shattering news came through, that Crassus had
been utterly defeated and slain at a great battle against the

Parthians at Carrhae. Desperately Caesar tried to heal the rift with Pompey by offering him as a new wife his great niece Octavia, but Pompey chose instead the widow of Publius Crassus who had been killed along with his father at Carrhae. She was the daughter of Metellus Scipio, one of Cato's strongest supporters in the Senate.

It was increasingly difficult for Caesar to manipulate things the way he wanted them in Rome. Through his friends Gaius Oppius and Cornelius Balbus in Rome he managed to buy a piece of land between the Capitol and the Senate House and there organized the construction of a splendid new forum, the Forum Julii, much of which stands today. It was to be a memorial to his conquest of Gaul and the cost was to come out of the riches he had so far acquired. It was also to be a source of work, and therefore of wages, to a great many people in Rome. This might be one way to keep some at least of the people on his side.

But before he could commemorate he had to win, and in 52 there occurred the most serious threat to the whole project – rebellion throughout Gaul and led by one man, Vercingetorix, a young chief infinitely superior to any of those who had hitherto challenged the might of Rome. All of a sudden the Gauls found a unity such as they had never known. Vercingetorix – the very name rings of the daring leadership which characterized this head of the Arverni tribe – aimed at no less than the total expulsion of the Romans from Gaul. Operating from a headquarters at Gergovia, Vercingetorix issued the call to arms. Within weeks half the tribes in Gaul had answered and acknowledged him their leader.

News of the rising reached Caesar in Italy in February 52, and he responded swiftly. Vercingetorix had banked on having the spring to organize the revolt properly, but Caesar, never daunted by obstacles natural or man-made, brought a small force across the Alps. They had to cut their way step by step through the snow which was then at its deepest and most frozen. In a few days he reached his legions and assembled them at Agedincum (Sens). After this things happened in quick succession.

Caesar was determined to get to the Arvernian capital, Gergovia. He marched down from Agedincum to Avaricum which he besieged and captured after a month. Vercingetorix withdrew to Gergovia with the bulk of his army and settled down to wait for Caesar to lay siege for him. Caesar brought six legions and an impressive assemblage of siege equipment, but despite a violent assault he failed to break in and had to retire. Then he marched south east and joined up with Labienus. Vercingetorix attacked them on the march but was repulsed. So he withdrew to the mountain of Alesia in the hope that Caesar would besiege him, and fail again. He started to fortify Alesia and at the same time sent for help from all his Gallic allies. Soon, nearly a quarter of a million Gauls were converging upon Alesia from all directions. Inside the town were another 80,000 men, with their women and children.

Caesar was never one to be caught twice. He ordered his legions to throw up an enormous earthwork around the hill on which Alesia stood. It was over eleven miles long, with two dozen turrets and eight camps for legionaries and horsemen. The earthworks, as he described them, consisted of three lines. The front line was a 20 ft wide trench, with upright sides. Behind this, some 650 yards away, were two more lines of trenches, equally deep, each 15 ft wide. The inner one was filled with water provided by diverting nearby streams. Behind the two trenches was a palisaded rampart about 12 ft high, with large forked branches sticking out to hinder besiegers who tried to clamber over. While this amazing set of defences was being constructed, Caesar heard of the approach of the massive conglomeration of Gallic tribes. So he ordered another series of earthworks to be built outside the first. These were similarly designed but longer by some three miles. His legions, of about 50,000 men, could thus take care of attack from both sides.

Vercingetorix and his Gauls imagined that they had Caesar completely sandwiched and that his destruction would be easy. They greatly underestimated him. The signal was given and the Gauls charged against the Romans on both sides. All day long the battle raged, over an area nearly half a mile wide and between eleven and fourteen miles in circumference. Here and there the Romans appeared to be yielding, but bold as ever and indifferent to personal safety, Caesar rode or walked from unit to unit, his general's scarlet cloak fluttering in the breeze for all his men to see, urging them on, until towards eventide the Gauls broke and fled. Vercingetorix had watched the final break up of his forces and thus the end of all his ambitions, and he accepted the position with calmness. He ordered envoys to go to Caesar and surrender on his behalf. Caesar accepted, and sent him as a prisoner to Rome. The vanquished Gauls were pardoned and sent home. The great danger was over, and all that remained was to suppress the last pockets of revolt in Gaul.

It had been a long, exhausting and murderous campaign. It had taken eight years. At the end of it Caesar had reached his half century and must have felt a lot older. But Gaul was secure. Not only did the Gauls stay loyal to him throughout the Civil War which was to follow, and throughout the years after Caesar's death when his great nephew Octavius struggled to consolidate his reconstruction work in the empire, they remained the staunchest of all the Roman provincials right to the last years of the empire in the 5th century AD. They had fought Caesar and they had lost. And when they yielded, their rebelliousness changed to affection and reverence. He gave many of them Roman citizenship and they rewarded him by naming many of their children after him. Within a century there were Gauls actually sitting as members of the Senate in Rome. The conquest of Gaul changed the Roman empire from a Mediterranean power to a European power, and therein lay the foundations of the Western Europe we know to-day.

NORTH SEA

N

BRITAIN
St. Albans
Wheathampstead

Canterbury Sandwich
Romney
Boulogne

Liege
Charleroi

Agedincum

GAUL

Vesontio

Alesia
(52 B.C.)

Vercellae
(101 B.C.)

Gergovia

Arausio
(107 B.C.)

Aquae Sextiae
(102 B.C.)

TRANSALPINE
GAUL

200 m
320 km

?........... Any comment author?

VII

CIVIL WAR

What was it that enabled Caesar to win and keep the respect, the admiration and the love of his troops for so long, through so many hardships? It is important to answer this question because soon after the conquest of Gaul Caesar had to ask them to invade their own country, Italy, to uphold his honour, and because when he asked them they responded willingly.

The secret of Caesar's popularity with his troops was two-fold: he was one of them and he seemed to have some magic star protecting him. He often called it his 'destiny'.[1] Despite his patrician background, his dandified dress and appearance, his long political career, his intimacy with the greatest men of Rome, he would muck in with the troops easily, unaffectedly, wholeheartedly, whatever the circumstances. He was as good a swordsman as the best of them. He could outride any of his cavalrymen. He could – and frequently did – sleep rough, under the stars with no cover. If food was short he would give up his rations to others. He could march with his men for hours, days, weeks, if need be, and never show any signs of

[1] Napoleon Bonaparte, the Emperor of the French, whose career in many ways resembled Caesar's, also believed in his own destiny and so did his troops.

fatigue. He was always up at the front in battle and on many occasions saved the day by leaping forward to head a charge. He took no chance with his army that he had not calculated as far as possible in advance. He led them into no ambushes. If they were frightened, he rallied them. When they were brave he praised them. Although he expected much from them he asked for nothing that he would not have been prepared to give himself.

On the march or in battle Caesar was stern and just with his troops. When they were off duty they could do more or less as they pleased. After a victory he would allow them extensive licence. 'Even if they do reek of scent' he used to say, 'my troops are crack fighters.' When he addressed them he called them 'Comrades'. He went to enormous trouble to boost their morale. Their weapons were expensively made; some indeed were inlaid with silver or gold. Just as with his political extravaganzas his gestures towards the troops were always well thought out, generous, sensational sometimes, and invariably ones that were not easily forgotten. One can easily imagine a couple of old Gallic campaigners reminiscing in a Roman tavern about the way the 'old man' gave such a beano after the Vercingetorix business.

There was another thing – speed, speed of decision, speed of action, speed in changing his plans. The enemy could never be sure what he was going to do next. He continually caught them unawares, as he did at Geneva (page *106*). As for his men, they, too, did not always know what was in his mind, but they trusted him absolutely. Now and again he acted with rashness, but the only engagements which he could be said to have lost were the siege of Gergovia and the attack of Dyrrachium (page *141*). Even those temporary setbacks were more than compensated by brilliant victories. Such swiftness was wasted unless his men were disciplined to respond to it, to sudden

A section from the Emperor Trajan's column in Rome. It shows the emperor (third from left) chatting to his troops before battle. Caesar always talked to his men before leading them into action.

orders or changes of orders. To keep them alert he used to make them turn out in full battle dress on all sorts of unnecessary occasions, like public holidays, wet days and so on. They were superbly drilled, reaching a pitch of discipline, courage and endurance unequalled anywhere. Invariably the numbers they defeated were many times larger than their own.

All of these things convinced his men that above everything else he cared for their welfare and, where possible, their safety. In return they devoted themselves, many of them their lives, to his service, and this made them extraordinarily brave and fearless. It also made them invincible. The historian Suetonius says that in the Civil War not one of his men deserted him. Only one officer crossed over to the other side, and that was Labienus. History has not told us why Labienus did desert, but we may guess at the reasons. He had been a friend of Pompey for a generation. He had never lost a battle in Gaul and so may have thought he was a better general than Caesar. Above all he may have resented the favours Caesar was increasingly bestowing on Mark Antony and Curio whom he found much more congenial companions. When he left Gaul, no reproach was heard from Caesar who sent all his personal luggage on.

Caesar's personal magnetism cannot alone explain this devotion. The men must also have been convinced of the rightness of his cause, even if it did mean involving Rome in bitter civil war. However illegal it was for him to invade his own land to take power by force, nothing can hide the fact that in doing so he had the complete support of nearly forty thousand of the best troops in the world. According to Suetonius, every centurion of every legion offered to equip a cavalryman out of his savings, and the legionaries unanimously volunteered to serve under him without pay or rations, pooling their money so that no one should go short.

Caesar's decision to march on Rome must be considered

with these facts in mind. They do not make the march any less illegal, but they certainly make it easier to understand.

After the death of Crassus and the collapse of the Triumvirate, things went from bad to worse in Rome. Candidates for the consulship were so unsuitable that in 52 Pompey was elected sole consul. Clodius was murdered by the gangs of Milo and the Senate House was burnt down in the rioting which followed. The Optimates, led by Cato, Ahenobarbus and Marcus Marcellus (consul for 51) now openly demanded the recall of Caesar from Gaul and made it known they would prosecute him for his acts of 59 BC. Instead of according Caesar and his splendid victorious troops who had added more than a quarter of a million square miles to the empire the honours they deserved, they wanted to brand him a public enemy.

At first, Pompey would not commit himself to joining the Optimates. Over the years they had consistently opposed him and it had not been solely because he was allied with Caesar. Indeed, he supported a bill put forward by the tribunes allowing Caesar to stand for the consulship in 49 for the year 48, without his having to give up his army. But it was clear to Caesar that it could not be long before Pompey drifted into the Optimate camp. His vanity would not long accept the fact that there was, north of the Italian border, a general whose exploits had equalled his, perhaps excelled them. Caesar therefore took steps to strengthen his own position, and for this he drew upon the vast reserves of money he had acquired through his conquest of Gaul. He planned to hold magnificent festivities to mark the death of Julia and word of these was allowed to filter back to the Roman populace, with glittering details of the intended gladiatorial fights, the public banquets and the cash presents. He continued with his great building programme in Rome and also commissioned works in various provinces.

In the political arena Caesar secured the support of several former opponents, particularly Gaius Scribonius Curio, the tribune, whose talents as mob orator and organizer were hardly less effective than Clodius'. Curio was won over by a promise to discharge his debts – some £100,000 worth of them. Another ally was Marcus Antonius (Mark Antony) who had been quaestor in 52 in Gaul. He had grown to love Caesar and no financial inducement was needed. And there were many others, some of whom genuinely believed Caesar to be the victim of pointless and unreasonable persecution. The political scene had by now become divided into three camps, the supporters of Caesar who saw that the republic must be drastically altered, those who would fight to the end to preserve what they were pleased to call the constitution, and those who felt anything from concern to indifference about one or other side but who would not commit themselves to any positive action.

The situation was a very fluid one. Prominent people changed sides for one reason or another. The consul for 50, Lucius Aemilius Paullus (brother of Marcus Aemilius Lepidus who was to be Caesar's Master of the Horse) had overspent on rebuilding the Basilica Aemilia in the Forum. Caesar underwrote the debt and Paullus went over to his side. Cicero, hitherto a tacit supporter of Caesar since the Luca conference of 56, now seemed to be drifting into the Optimate camp. What would Caesar and Pompey do?

The first signs that Pompey was beginning to turn on his old colleague came in the spring of 50. Following the defeat of Crassus in 53, the Parthians were threatening to invade the Roman province of Syria. The Senate authorized that Caesar and Pompey should release a legion each. Pompey decided to send a legion which he had lent Caesar after the 14th legion had been destroyed by Ambiorix in 54 (page *121*). This meant

that Caesar, having to send one of his own, was losing two.
Then Pompey was taken very ill while on a visit to Naples.
This gave Caesar's allies time to block moves in the Senate
preventing him from retaining his command in Gaul and still
be allowed to stand for the consulship.

In the election of the summer of 50, some of Caesar's
supporters won offices. His wife's father, Piso, became one
of the censors. Mark Antony and Quintus Cassius Longinus
were both elected tribunes, which would ensure continuity
of support for Caesar from the tribunate (Curio was tribune
for 50), and these could veto Senate proposals. But opposition
was building up, and as it did, the language of the Optimates
towards Caesar became more violent. This was in sharp
contrast to his restrained and moderate attitude. When the
Senate demanded he should disband his legions, he said
politely that he would do so gladly provided Pompey did
likewise. He did not need an army if there was no army
against him. He was confident that he could carry through
all the reforms he wanted as consul.

Pompey now recovered from his illness and this became
the occasion for thanksgiving all over Italy. It led him to
suppose that the country looked to him to solve the political
crisis. And so the country did, but he made the mistake of
thinking that the people meant him to desert Caesar altogether
and join up with the Optimates. It was perhaps at this time
that Titus Labienus, Caesar's second-in-command in Gaul
and his trusted friend of many years, opened negotiations
with Pompey and the Optimates about changing sides.

In December 50 the Senate, nearly all of whose members
were most anxious to preserve peace at almost any cost voted
by an overwhelming majority (370 to 22) that both Caesar
and Pompey should retire from their commands. Then, to
the consternation of the whole city, the consul Marcellus led

those Optimates who had voted against the proposal out to Pompey at his palace not far from Rome. There they asked him to defend the state. They issued the ultimate decree, and it was done without the knowledge or approval of the great majority of the Senate. To make matters worse they gave him as extra troops the two legions which should have gone to Syria.

Caesar was alarmed at what he heard. So he sent for his forces from Gaul. He stationed three legions in Transalpine Gaul to protect his rear from Pompey's Spanish army. One legion he concentrated at Ravenna, on the border of Italy. Two more he held in reserve. Then he sent conciliatory messages to the Senate that he would give up his province, retaining only two legions until he should be elected consul. But of course it was the consulship his enemies were bent on preventing. The Senate replied probably at the dictation of Cato, that no accommodation could be made with him. He must give up his legions. Caesar retaliated with a big propaganda campaign through speeches and pamphlets via his agents that the State was in the hands of a small minority bent on destroying him, even if it meant bringing down the republic. He 'stood for the free expression of their (the people's) will by the Senate and the popular assembly'.

On 7th January 49 the Senate resolved that Caesar should be declared a public enemy unless he laid down his command. This was the same Senate that a few weeks ago had voted that both he and Pompey should resign. How the majority was swung against Caesar, in spite of the efforts of the tribunes Mark Antony and Cassius to veto the proposal, is not known. Quite probably alarming stories about his aims, of how he would loose his legions on Rome in an orgy of massacre like Marius and Sulla, were deliberately circulated.

The news of the resolution reached Caesar very quickly,

probably the day after, as he was now at Ravenna on the border. It called for prompt action and without hesitation he took it. Half a legion was sent across the Rubicon,[1] the dividing line between Cisalpine Gaul and Italy proper, to capture the town of Ariminum. The other half was ordered to take Arretium in Etruria. These were all the troops he had at the moment. He knew perfectly well that he was starting a civil war, but he had endured more provocation than any Roman before him. And he was confident that he would win. His luck, that element which had played a not inconsiderable part in his career, would not desert him.[2]

Once he had crossed the Rubicon, Caesar hoped to add to the consternation in Rome by pushing downwards into Italy on a narrow front as fast as he could. What he could not do with numbers he would do with surprise, and long distances covered in a few days always impressed people. And so it happened. Neither Pompey nor the Senate had expected him to move without his full army. His supreme qualities of speed and resolution completely outwitted them. They might have been willing to re-open negotiations, as again Caesar asked, but, intransigent as ever, Cato talked them out of it. Instead, they called upon Pompey to produce the legions he once said would rise to his call at the stamp of his foot.

Caesar pressed on, greatly encouraged by the number of towns that opened their gates to him – to find he treated the inhabitants with kindness and mercy. Ancona, Auximum, Cingulum (which had been endowed with a large sum by Labienus but which nonetheless elected to join Caesar), Asculum, all fell in a few days. In Rome the Optimates were

[1] We may discount the story that Caesar hesitated on the banks of the Rubicon, tossing a coin, weighing up whether he should cross or not.

[2] Caesar really had no alternative. If he laid down his command and returned to Rome as a private individual, he would certainly have been arrested, tried, and executed by his enemies, in other words, judicially murdered.

Roman legionary at the time of the Civil War

thrown into confusion, and only Pompey kept his head. The city must be evacuated, he said, and the war carried over into Greece where he could count, he thought, on considerable support. And when he left for Brundisium, he was followed by all the Optimates except Cicero who believed (rightly) that he had nothing to fear. Behind them came large numbers of uncommitted senators who had been bullied into abandoning the capital by threats of what would happen to them when Pompey crushed Caesar, if they stayed. Pompey had been persuaded, unwisely, to state that all who were not with him were against him. When Caesar heard this he countered by announcing that all who were not against him were free to consider themselves his supporters. He gathered up a force and raced down to intercept Pompey, reaching Brundisium just as Pompey was about to embark for Greece. Once more Caesar tried to parley, but it was too late. The ships sailed out of the harbour. The civil war had begun.

Caesar wasted no more time. He turned back to Rome. On the way he called on Cicero at his villa in Formiae. Would Cicero come to Rome to speak in the Senate on his behalf, Caesar asked. Cicero said he could not. So Caesar went on and as soon as he reached the city walls (he could not go in as he was still a general in command of an army) he asked the Senate to come to a meeting outside. It was a poor turn out. Most of those whose presence would have given it any kind of authority had left with Pompey. True, the tribunes Antony and Cassius were there, giving the meeting a legality, but there were no consuls. Caesar spoke to the senators and invited them to support him in running the government. And then a note of impatience crept into his words – if they did not want to help, then he would govern on his own. He spoke to the Assembly of the people in the same vein, promising a distribution of corn and a free cash hand-out. For the latter he needed money and there followed a disagreeable incident in which his impatience again predominated.

He had learned that there was, in the treasury vaults of the temple of Saturn, a huge reserve of gold and silver bars and coins of gold, silver and copper.[1] The Senate was persuaded to grant him the use of this money, but when he went with some troops to fetch it, one of the tribunes, Lucius Caecilius Metellus, stopped him. Caesar was irritated and threatened to have Metellus put to death. This incident damaged his image with the people whom he had been assiduously courting for so long, and most of the authorities say he left Rome in a great hurry to avoid unpleasantness.

Now that Italy was in his hands, Caesar set out, not as his enemies expected for Greece, but for Spain where some of Pompey's legions were waiting to be sent for. These had to be knocked out. As Caesar put it, 'I am going to fight an army without a general, and then I shall fight a general without an army.' At the same time he sent Quintus Valerius Orca to Sardinia and Curio to Sicily, to secure these corn-producing islands. In Rome he left the praetor Marcus Aemilius Lepidus in charge of the government, and his friend Mark Antony in command of the remaining troops in Italy.

His campaign in Spain was short and victorious, and very few lives were lost. When he was on his way back to Italy he heard that Curio, having won Sicily, crossed over to North Africa and was defeated and slain by Juba, king of Numidia, who had sided with the Optimates. Publius Cornelius Dolabella, whom he had left in command of his ships in the Adriatic Sea, had been driven back to harbour by a Pompeian fleet. And then the 9th Legion had mutinied. It was a sorry list of disasters. Caesar decided to deal sternly with the mutiny.

---

[1] The amount was about 15,000 gold bars, 30,000 silver bars and £1M in cash.

He ordered one man in every ten to be arrested and executed, as was the Roman habit in mutinies, though before allowing the sentences to be carried out he reduced the number to twelve individual ring-leaders.

Sometime on his journey back to Italy he received notification from Lepidus that the Assembly had appointed him dictator. Caesar was delighted to get this news, for it meant that he could now authorize the holding of consular elections for 48. This was extremely important to him; he had said, ever since the trouble with the Optimates began, that he wanted the consulship by constitutional means. The civil war was being fought over his right to stand as much as over anything else. If he could win the election legally, it would show that in Italy at all events he was the man the majority wanted as head of the government. Pompey had abdicated his rights by leaving the country and raising war in the provinces.

Caesar arrived in Rome and at once held consular elections which he won, with Publius Servilius Isauricus (son of the Isauricus who had been his commander in 78 BC) as colleague. He also saw to it that most of the other magistracies were filled by candidates sympathetic to his cause. Ancient historians agree that he spent only eleven days in the city but in that time conducted a considerable amount of business. The biggest problem was the economy. Men waited to see whether he would cancel all debts, as some feared, and plunder the rich to balance the country's books. He was more sensible than that. All debts were to be paid but the interest paid on them to the date of his pronouncement was to be regarded as part of the repayment. Where land or houses were used for paying, they were to be valued at what they were worth before his break with Pompey, which was higher. That way both creditors and debtors felt they had not been too badly let down.

Caesar gave Roman citizenship to the Italians north of the river Po, thus fulfilling the promise he made them in 59 (page 96). He restored full rights to those families who had been proscribed by Sulla in 82 (page 59). On the eleventh day he laid down the dictatorship and headed for Brundisium. There, his army was waiting, ready to embark for Epirus in Greece. The next day, 20,000 legionaries and about 600 cavalry landed near Palaeste in what is now Albania. They had completely surprised Pompey who thought Caesar would not attempt a landing until the spring. Immediately, Caesar advanced upwards in the direction of Dyrrachium where Pompey's army was based. When he reached the river Apsus he pitched camp and sent a delegation to try once more to parley with Pompey. It was no use; Labienus, now Pompey's leading general, ended the discussions with the curt remark: 'Stop this talk of agreement. Peace is impossible for us without the delivery of Caesar's head.'

Mark Antony, meanwhile, had managed to bring reserve legions across the sea and had landed at Lissus, about 50 miles north of Dyrrachium. He joined up with Caesar and together they converged upon Pompey's camp which was fortified by about 14 miles of entrenchments. Before attacking it they threw up their own earthworks, some 17 miles long, which Caesar believed would contain the Pompeian forces. For a while both sides stayed behind their fortifications, enduring shortages of food. The hunger was worse in Caesar's camp for it was too early for a harvest and there was no grain to be had. So he ordered loaves to be made of a root not unlike grass. Such was the stamina of his men that they lived on these for weeks. One loaf was seized by a Pompeian raiding party, and shown to Pompey who exclaimed: 'I am fighting wild beasts. Hide it at once.' He knew well that the morale of his men would sag if they saw how resolute their enemies were.

Roman legionaries attacking a fortress in testudo formation, that is, with shields locked together to form a protective shell against defenders' missiles. Testudo means tortoise, and the picture shows well why the Romans called this formation a tortoise.

Then, one night, Pompey sent a detachment to make a surprise attack at the southern end of Caesar's fortifications. They broke through, overpowered a part of Caesar's army and then – instead of wheeling round and attacking the main lines of Caesar's army from behind – they stood still. As Caesar said afterwards 'Pompey could have won the war to-day if he had known how to command.' It had been a grievous fight, and it was the second defeat of Caesar's career. But, as he had at Gergovia in 52, he turned the defeat into ultimate victory. Within three weeks Pompey was offering battle in the plain of Pharsalus, with nearly 50,000 men against Caesar's 20,000. Labienus had filled his head with stories of how Caesar's men were overtired, sick, unpaid and ready to collapse. They were no longer the brave legionaries with which he had conquered Gaul. Caesar's defeat was certain.

Caesar was delighted; he, too, wanted a decision by battle. He placed his army alongside a small river which covered his left flank. Then he spoke to his men, calling for more effort for his honour and theirs. He told them to use their javelins as swords at close quarters and to aim at enemy faces. As Pompey's cavalry charged down upon Caesar's right flank they suddenly came upon a sea of upward thrusting spikes. It was too much and they broke and scattered. Caesar ordered his men to advance and in a few hours they rolled back Pompey's infantry lines and chased them off the field through their camp and beyond. By next morning over 25,000 had surrendered, but to Caesar's horror, nearly 15,000 lay dead on the battlefield. As he gazed at their bodies he gave way to grief at the senseless loss of Roman lives. 'They brought it on themselves. They would have it so. I, Caius Caesar, should have been condemned despite all my achievements, had I not appealed to my army for help.' The losses on his side were small indeed, about 250, but of these 30 were centurions, all brave leaders of men. One was the veteran Caius Crastinus. This wonderful old soldier had cried out before the battle began, 'Follow me, old comrades, and give your general the good service you have always given. When we have won this battle we shall regain our liberty and Caesar his proper place in the state.' And to his general he said: 'I shall make you want to thank me today, whether I am alive or dead at the end of it.' And so he did, and fell at the head of his troops, cut to pieces with sword wounds. Caesar had his body searched for, decorated with military honours and buried apart from the rest.

When he reached Pompey's camp, Caesar found that his adversary had gone, swift as the wind on horseback, heading for Egypt where, perhaps, he dreamed of leading once more an army against his conqueror.

After the battle, Caesar displayed the clemency for which he has become famous. He spared the Pompeian troops and also those of their officers who had not fled to remote parts of the empire to make trouble for him in the years to come. This clemency of Caesar's, so famous that a special coin was struck to commemorate it, has been questioned. Was it the expression of a generous soul, a feature of a rare chivalry? Or was it sheer policy, calculated to win friends on the way to the summit of power? Certainly the Pompeians feared massacres like those of Marius and Sulla, and they justified them by recalling the cruelties Caesar had committed in Gaul.[1] In this they were no doubt influenced by Cato who refused to look for any good whatever in Caesar. But if Caesar had been moved to clemency only by policy, he could not have spared his enemies so often (as he did), many of whom in the end joined together to kill him.

Caesar may have defeated Pompey in the field but he did not underestimate him or his powers of recovery and he decided to pursue him. The matter had to be settled once and for all, so he followed on to Egypt. When he sailed into Alexandria harbour he was met by a deputation from the joint sovereign of this semi-independent kingdom, the boy king Ptolemy XIII. He was handed a package which when it was unwrapped contained, to his horror, the severed and

---

[1] At the end of the war in Gaul a band of some thousands of outlaws held out for a long time in the town of Uxellodunum against a siege. When the town fell, Caesar punished the survivors by cutting off their right hands.

embalmed head of Pompey. For a few moments Caesar wept and then turned away in disgust. How had great Pompey come to so miserable an end as this? Then he learned what had happened. When Pompey had reached Alexandria only a few days earlier he had stepped ashore from a boat to be greeted by Achillas, Ptolemy's chief general, and some Roman officers. He thanked them for the welcome, and then swung round to help his wife out of the boat. As his back was turned, one of the officers, Septimius, plunged a sword in his back, and the great man fell face down into the wet sand, the sea reddening with his blood.

This was not the way Caesar wanted the resolution of the civil war. This was not how he squared his enemies. And he could not forget that Pompey and he had been bound together through Julia. This appalling introduction to Egypt was to colour his dealings with Egyptian politicians in the weeks to come.

Egypt was ruled jointly by Ptolemy XIII and his sister Cleopatra VII, who were children when their father died in 51 BC. The kingdom had been left under the guardianship of Rome. It was a rich land and it provided enough corn for a third of Rome's needs for a year. It also produced paper, glass, linen, jewellery and scents which Rome wanted in quantity. When Caesar arrived in Alexandria the two monarchs had fallen out and were at war. Caesar invited both to come to meet him to settle their differences. They came, though Cleopatra thought it amusing to have herself smuggled in. She was twenty-one, attractive if not beautiful, clever, witty, and for her age well versed in politics. She had heard of Caesar's reputation as a lover – who had not? – and she determined to win a settlement in her favour by exercising her charms.

Achillas seized control of the king's army and blockaded

A coin bearing a portrait of Cleopatra, queen of Egypt. The sculptor evidently did not consider her to have been very glamorous.

Caesar in Alexandria. Caesar sent for help to an old ally in Asia Minor, Mithradates, king of Pergamum, an illegitimate son of the great Pontine enemy of Rome, Mithradates VI. Meanwhile, he fended as best he could under siege conditions. The Egyptians poisoned his water supply, so he dug fresh wells. They tried to get to their ships, so he set fire to them. Then he tried to get closer to them by taking to a boat in the harbour. But the boat was overturned by Egyptian divers and Caesar was thrown into the water. He swam ashore to safety only with the greatest difficulty as he had to keep one hand above the water clutching important papers. Eventually the Egyptians called off the siege and Caesar managed to join his army outside.

Mithradates, with an army containing a contingent of Jews, arrived and between them he and Caesar defeated the Egyptians somewhere not far from modern Cairo in a battle in which Ptolemy was drowned. The crown passed to Cleo-

patra and her younger brother, Ptolemy XIV. This was at the
end of March in 47. Two weeks later Caesar left Egypt for
Asia Minor to deal with Pharnaces, another son of Pontine
Mithradates, who was reviving his father's ambitions.

If Caesar and Cleopatra did enjoy a wild love affair involving
a prolonged cruise up the Nile to see the monuments of the
pharaohs, as has been suggested, they would have had to pack
it into that fortnight. But no evidence of any kind has come
down from his time to bear out the romantic legends of the
ageing conqueror being so bewitched by the young and
beautiful queen that he abandoned his responsibilities for
months.

When he left Egypt he proceeded to Judaea (Palestine) with
a small force and there he rewarded the Jews for their help by
allowing them to rebuild the walls of Jerusalem (partially
destroyed by Pompey in the 60s) and by conferring Roman
citizenship on Herod Antipater, their ruler. Hastening on to
Pontus he confronted Pharnaces at Zela (Zilleh) and there on
1st August inflicted a crushing defeat upon him. Pharnaces
had actually ordered his chariots to charge uphill at Caesar's
ranks! He fled from the field and was murdered shortly
afterwards.

This was the victory which Caesar described to his friend
Caius Matius in Rome in a message which read: 'Veni, Vidi,
Vici' – 'I came, I saw, I conquered.'

Caesar had not seen Italy for about 18 months. It was by
any standards a long time for a ruler to be away from his capital,
and in his case the risks were all the greater because many of the
Optimate leaders had survived Pharsalus and were planning
a big come-back in North Africa. What had happened in
Italy?

Scarcely a month after Pharsalus, Caesar had been created
dictator again, but in his absence (September 48), and Mark

Antony had been appointed master of his horse, that is, dictator's deputy. The news of Pompey's death reached Rome by the end of the year. It was the signal for a veritable flood of honours and powers to descend upon his conqueror from a Senate which perhaps was feeling an overwhelming sense of relief. Caesar was granted the power to make war or peace on behalf of Rome without having to consult either the Senate or the Assembly. He could hold the consulship for five years running. He could be a tribune at the same time. He could decide who should stand for the other magistracies. He could nominate the governors of the provinces. These were the most absolute powers hitherto held by any Roman. In Caesar's hands they need not have been dangerous, but when they were in Mark Antony's, as his deputy, they were being abused, destroying much of the goodwill so patiently built up by Caesar. There was rioting and street fighting; the days of Clodius and Milo were back. Some of the younger politicians were agitating for cancelling all debts. The land-owners and businessmen were frightened. And the troops in Italy were getting restive. Where was their general? When was he going to triumph? Could they be discharged now? And what about the rewards promised so long ago?

Caesar arrived at Tarentum at the end of September 47 and headed for Rome. He was hardly through the gate when he summoned a meeting of the Senate. He had sized up the situation accurately. Mark Antony had a heart of gold, but he was irresponsible, greedy and boorish, and not the right man to deputize for a dictator in a land where every move was being watched by those who had yet to decide whether to throw in their lot with him. Caesar dismissed him from office, though not from his circle of friends, and appointed Lepidus in his place. His debt law of 49 was restated but with some modifications to produce rent reductions on houses. Then he

N

Byzantium
BITHYNIA   PONTUS
Troy
Mitylene
•Zela
(47 B.C.)
•Carrhae
(53 B.C.)
SYRIA
Rhodes
CRETE
JUDAEA
Jerusalem
PARTHIA
Alexandria
EGYPT
RED SEA
240 m
380 km

set out to meet the restive troops, among them the 10th Legion, his favoured legion in Gaul. They had assembled on the Campus Martius, a battle training ground just outside the walls of Rome, lying on a bend of the Tiber.

Caesar walked up towards their ranks, alone and unguarded, and raised his hand. 'Citizens,' he cried out, for they were no longer soldiers so far as he was concerned. As the word went down the ranks the full import of it struck home in every heart. And when it had, the murmurings of discontent changed to cries of protest at such humiliation. At once their leaders came forward and craved, abjectly, for forgiveness. Caesar shrugged his shoulders and muttered some disparaging remarks. They pleaded all the more, offering to sacrifice certain of their number for punishment. At last he yielded.

The time had come to set out for North Africa, but before he left there was still some business to attend to in Rome. He resigned the dictatorship again and assumed the consulship for 46, with Lepidus as his colleague. He filled up the membership of the Senate by giving seats to provincial businessmen, even to worthy centurions (perhaps he would have made Crastinus one had he lived). And he increased the number of praetors to ten, designating the officers in every case. The government was securely Caesarian as he left for what everyone believed was the final encounter with his enemies. One chilly December day he embarked from Ostia for Sicily where his legions were gathered by the harbour of Lilybaeum. A week later he gave the signal to depart and his ships drew anchor and sailed out. Inside their hulls were six legions, 2000 cavalry, and their supplies. Were these enough to finish off the Optimate resistance?

VIII

DICTATOR FOR LIFE

Four days after he left Lilybaeum, Caesar landed near Hadru-
metum on the North African coast, with 3000 legionaries
and 150 cavalry. The rest of his forces were spread out in the
other ships looking for suitable landing grounds nearby. As
he stepped out of the boat taking him ashore, Caesar stumbled
and fell. A gasp of horror went up from his troops, who
regarded it as a terrible omen. But Caesar, ever considerate
of his men's feelings, quickly turned this into a favourable
omen by hugging the sand and shouting 'Africa! I have tight
hold of you!'

His landing took his enemies by surprise: they were not
ready for him. And it was just as well, for his troops were
largely raw recruits and needed several weeks drill and training. While he organized this, Caesar mounted an extensive
propaganda campaign in North Africa offering promises of
freedom and cash incentives to all who would come over to
his cause. He was enormously helped by being the nephew of
Marius who had distributed land in North Africa to his
veterans, whose descendants still blessed his name. 'To the
magic of Marius' name Caesar added the magic of his own.'

Before long thousands of legionaries and native Africans deserted the Optimates or their ally, king Juba of Numidia. Whole cities came over to Caesar, and by April he was ready to take on his enemies. On the 4th, he directed his legions against the town of Thapsus which lay on the coast and which was held by the Optimates. The approach to it was across a narrow stretch of land between the sea and a marshy inland lake. An army led along this strip could easily be boxed in by blocking off both ends, and when Caesar was seen to lead his men along this road, the Optimate commander Metellus Scipio was delighted. His opponent had walked right into a trap. Once again, however, the Optimates had underestimated him. Caesar had deliberately chosen this route in the confident hope that the Optimates would try to entrap him, for this would mean dividing their forces and so weakening the overall command of the situation.

While Scipio blocked off the north and Juba the south, Caesar formed his legions in two flanks. The men were impatient to attack and did not heed his signal to wait. They charged down the strip in both directions and routed the divided enemy forces. Then the pent-up hatred of the legionaries for these unyielding opponents of their hero, held in check ever since the crossing of the Rubicon, burst forth and manifested itself in a frightful massacre of the enemy, many of whom were in fact quite ready to surrender. No quarter was granted; ten thousand, most of them Romans, were butchered. When Caesar's officers tried to stop the slaughter, the men turned on them, too.

The Optimate cause was broken. Scipio, Juba and other leaders were dead. Labienus escaped with two of Pompey's sons, Cnaeus and Sextus. Cato survived, but he robbed Caesar of the opportunity of pardoning him by committing suicide. He had been left in command of the town of Utica

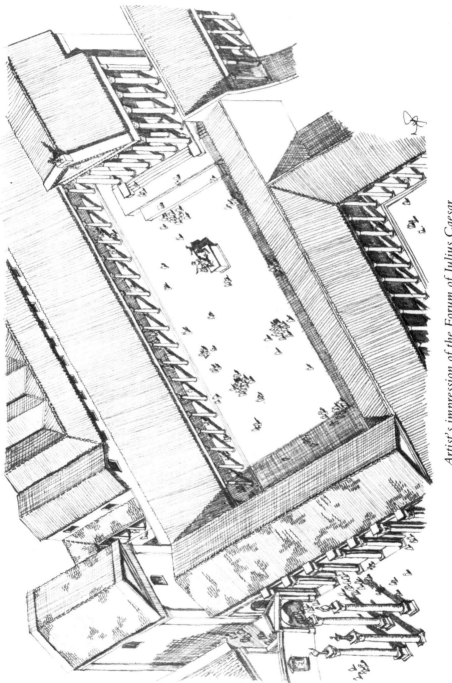

Artist's impression of the Forum of Julius Caesar

and when the Roman residents decided to surrender, Cato took his own life. The residents were spared but forced to pay a huge fine. So were many other cities. The area was then reorganized, new colonies founded[1] and the grain and olive oil industries were re-activated. Soon, North Africa was making a sizeable contribution of both to the capital.

Caesar did not return to Italy until July of 46. The news of his victory at Thapsus preceded him and it was the signal for a fresh outpouring of honours: a supplicatio of forty days (imagine it – nearly six weeks!); the dictatorship for ten years; prefect of morals for three years (the combined offices of two censors rolled into one); the right to sit between the consuls at any Senate meeting and to speak first at any debate; a statue of him with the globe at his feet to be set up inside the Capitoline temple; and many more. Some of these Caesar must surely have suspected as being deliberately over-flattering. The active Optimates in the empire may have been crushed, but there were still senators in Rome who did not like the concentration of power in his hands. There was Cicero whose letters of the time contained remarks like 'we are slaves to him and he himself to the times'. And there were younger men like Brutus and Caius Cassius Longinus who had been pardoned Pompeians and now held high office through Caesar's magnanimity and yet who harboured notions of 'restoring the republic', an ideal that was meaningless in the context of the times.

When Caesar at last reached Rome he was able to begin tackling the great mass of political, social and administrative problems which had been piling up. These can be summed up in the phrase 'the need to reconstruct the machinery of government'. They were far more than a man of even his consum-

---

[1]Carthage, destroyed in 146BC by the Romans (page 32), was rebuilt at about this time by Caesar and made into a colony.

mate genius could manage, and yet in the two years left to him before he was killed he accomplished enough to astonish historians of all shades of opinion ever since. What these historians do not agree about is whether he was consciously trying to solve the overall problem or whether he was just producing spontaneous solutions to individual difficulties. The key to the argument perhaps lies in what his great friend, Caius Matius, said after his death. 'If Caesar with all his genius could not find a way out, who will find one now?'

Some of the best biographers of Caesar have taken this to mean that Caesar made no attempt to solve this great reconstruction problem, and it is probably the dominating view in academic circles[1] today. But I believe this to be a misinterpretation of what Matius said. Clearly he meant that Caesar had tried and had not succeeded by the time of his assassination. But the settlement finally brought into being by his great-nephew Augustus, which Matius may not have lived to see, was Julius' achievement.

His overall aim, of which he made no secret, was quiet in Italy, peace in the provinces, and security and welfare in the empire. A look at some of his practical reforms may show the direction his mind was taking. He organized a census of the Roman population. The total is not known but is thought to have been not much under a million. Of these he found some 300,000 had been getting free hand-outs of grain; that is, about a third of the population had been living more or less on the state, idle, bored and unproductive. He cut this figure by half by instituting the equivalent of a means test and by encouraging thousands to go and settle in the new colonies he was creating or had already initiated.[2] Some 80,000

[1] Michael Grant: *Julius Caesar*. J. P. V. D. Balsdon: *Julius Caesar and Rome*.

[2] Greece, North Africa, Spain, Asia Minor, Transalpine Gaul.

were settled. Rioting and disturbances among the remainder in the city were discouraged when he banned political clubs, those hot-beds of revolution which as a younger man he had organized so skilfully as a political weapon. At the same time he bolstered up the city's population by admitting to citizenship new types of people, provincial businessmen, professional men like doctors, teachers, scientists and artists.

While improving the lot of the inhabitants of Rome he extended the privilege of Roman citizenship.[1] He enlarged the membership of the Senate from about 600 to about 900, and introduced people from the humblest backgrounds, even from the provinces, many as a reward for services to him in his climb to power. This provided him with a comfortable majority. Of course he insisted that they had the right qualifications. He regarded this injection of new blood into the Senate as a useful insurance against a return to the old predominance of the Optimates. Naturally, the remnants of these resented this expansion, but when all was said and done Caesar was only using the weapon their class had been employing for centuries to maintain their majority. In increasing the size of the Senate, however, he reduced its influence. He did not always feel obliged to consult it, and if he did it was often to obtain endorsement for something he had already intended to do. He began to rule more and more by edict and by putting proposals to the popular Assembly where there was generally a certainty that they would get carried.

Caesar conceived a number of far-reaching schemes, startling even by today's standards. A canal was to be cut across the Isthmus of Corinth to improve sea communications between Italy and the East. The Fucine lake and the Pomptine marshes, not far from Rome, were to be drained to produce

---

[1] The attempt to do this by Gaius Gracchus in 121 had led to his violent end (page 36).

more arable land. New trunk roads were to be built, including one from the Adriatic Sea across the Apennines down towards Rome. In the Campus Martius he planned to build the largest temple in the world, and the harbour at Ostia was to be greatly enlarged. He commissioned Marcus Terentius Varro to build a huge library and fill it with a copy of every book available in Greek and Latin. And he discussed with legal experts the codification of the civil law in one huge work.

No man had ever before dreamed up such a grandiose collection of schemes. They were a splendid manifestation of his boundless self-confidence, of his ability to think in world-embracing terms. But only one of them was actually started upon in his lifetime, the library scheme under Varro. The canal at Corinth was not cut until the end of the 19th century; the Fucine lake was drained by Claudius, nearly a century after Caesar, but the Pomptine marshes had to wait until the Italian dictator Mussolini did it in the 1930s; the harbour at Ostia was not enlarged until the time of Claudius, and the codification of the law was organized by the Byzantine emperor Justinian I (527–565).

One of his reforms, completed quickly, had benefits which are with the Western world today. This was the reorganization of the calendar. Up to this time the Roman year had been one of 355 days. Every second year an extra and shorter month of 22 or 23 days, alternately, was added at the end of February to provide an average year length of $366\frac{1}{4}$ days. The correct dating procedures were supposed to be managed by the college of pontiffs (of which Caesar was then head) but over the years the procedure had been neglected. The calendar on paper was two months out on the calendar of time. Caesar consulted the Greek astronomer Sosigenes and they decided that to make the year 45 start on the right day, the current year 46 must be extended to have 445 days. Thereafter, years

A British (Celtic) pot with relief decoration showing gladiators in the arena.

would be $365\frac{1}{4}$ days long, with an extra day each fourth year tacked on to the end of February.

Stunning though all these great schemes were, they were not the major topic of interest to the people of Rome in the summer of 46. When Caesar came back from Africa they were thinking of only one thing – the celebrations of his victories he had promised to hold. Knowing their Caesar they confidently expected them to be better than anything they had ever seen. And so they were. Four triumphs were the main feature of a ten-day programme of festivities, to celebrate the conquest of Gaul, the defeat of the Egyptians, the victory at Zela and the defeat of Juba (the victories of Pharsalus and Thapsus could not be celebrated: they were battles between Romans; nor, indeed, would Caesar have wished to do so.) Each one had its central publicity theme. The Gallic triumph, illustrated with placards commemorating his many victories, reached its climax in the appearance, in chains, of Vercingetorix who, after the parade was by Roman tradition executed. The victory in Egypt was highlighted by the display of Cleopatra's sister, Arsinoe, who had misguidedly taken the wrong side in the war between Cleopatra and Ptolemy XIII. She was released after the triumph; so, too, was the son of Juba, a young lad of four. The biggest laughs were raised in the triumphal parade to celebrate Zela which had placards showing Pharnaces running away.

Throughout the celebrations, as was customary in these things, his veteran soldiers chanted the rudest songs about their chief as he rode on a chariot drawn by white horses through the city, behind the procession of cars and floats. One of these was recorded so that Suetonius could write it down:

> Home we bring our bald whoremonger.
> Romans, lock your wives away.
> All the bags of gold you lent him
> Went his Gallic tarts to pay![1]

Caesar would have chuckled with the rest at this stanza; it summed him up in many eyes. They even sang about his so-called 'affair' with king Nicomedes of Bithynia, nearly forty years before (page 63).

And with the triumphs came the feasts, the dancing, the music, the entertainments and – most anxiously awaited of all – the money hand-outs. This was what the troops really wanted; £1000 cash for every legionary, £2000 for the centurions, £4000 for the officers. Even the civilian population who had done no fighting – except in the streets – got some

---

[1] Quoted verbatim from Robert Graves' wonderful translation of Suetonius' Twelve Caesars, Penguin Classics, 1957.

A reconstruction of the centre of Rome as it would have been if there had been no great fire in 64 AD. The tall building at left is the Theatre of Marcellus, which

was started by Caesar's architects. Among the colonnaded buildings at right is his Forum, opened in 46 BC.

gold coins as well as a liberal hand-out of corn and oil. And to keep the populace at the pitch of excitement he held games, seafights on artificial lakes, gladiatorial contests, wild beast shows including (for the first time) a giraffe, and an enormous public banquet at over 20,000 tables, better than anything Crassus had put on, with a promise of another later in the week, to celebrate the opening of his new Forum Julii which was now ready.

None of Caesar's reforms nor his building works could be carried out without help. He needed a government, and part of the credit for the success of his programme must be accorded to a number of friends of his who looked after the detailed administration of his schemes, and we may suppose brought him down to earth from time to time where any of them seemed impractical. These men had much in common, loyalty, efficiency, diligence, integrity and enthusiasm. Above all they were devoted to Caesar and considered it the summit of their ambition to serve him well. Those most close to him were Cornelius Balbus, Caius Oppius and Caius Matius, friends of long standing. They sought no high office, and only Balbus ever achieved one, the consulate, four years after Caesar's death. These loyal men began to construct a network of assistants forming a civil service which was to become indispensable to the emperors in succeeding generations.[1]

Even before the great triumphal celebrations were over, disturbing news had begun to arrive from Spain. There, young Cnaeus Pompey and Labienus had renewed the war and had succeeded in mustering a considerable army, composed chiefly of Spaniards who were not Roman citizens. Caesar was in

---

[1] It was the existence of this imperial civil service which kept the empire from disintegrating in many crises of its five centuries, most notably in the terrible seventy odd years from the death of Septimius Severus in 211 AD to the accession of Diocletian in 284.

some difficulties over raising troops himself. Many of his legions had been disbanded and the men settled in Italy or in the colonies. Even the 10th Legion was largely made up of volunteers. So he had to leave Italy and hope to pick up additional volunteers in Gaul and Spain. This time he was assured of support even from the conservative opposition in Rome. No one relished the prospect of a victory by Pompey who had none of the qualities of his great father, and whose reputation for savagery was about as bad as people like Ariovistus. Caius Cassius, soon to be nominated praetor, said at the time 'I would prefer to keep our mild old master than try out a cruel new one,' which was probably the general attitude of the opposition.

The war in Spain was short and bloody. The campaign, fought in the Sierra Nevada in the south, ended in a victory at Munda, about 50 miles east of Gades, on 17th March 45. There, both sides fought desperately, with none of the chivalry or the reluctance to kill fellow Romans which had characterized Pharsalus. At one point Caesar's line began to crumple. Immediately he leapt from his horse, seized a shield and rushed to the front shouting 'Aren't you ashamed to hand me over to these boys?'. Fired by his zeal, the troops held firm while Caesar sent in a cavalry arm against the enemy's right flank. Labienus saw this move, so typical of Caesar's reaction to a crisis in battle, and began to move men to meet the shock. But the rest of his army thought these men were abandoning the field and they began to run, too. At once Caesar's troops pursued them and cut them down in thousands. Among the dead was Labienus. True to his spirit of generosity Caesar ordered him to be buried with honour.[1]

---

[1] Cnaeus Pompey was caught afterwards and killed. There was no honourable burial for him. Caesar had his head fixed on a spike in Seville.

Caesar remained in Spain for some weeks to administer the province and organize new colonies of citizens from Rome and from Spain. Many of the settlements took names commemorating him, such as Julia Victrix Nova Carthago (New Carthage). These communities were granted their own mini-constitutions, with elective town councils, obligations for military service, and so forth. They were in fact municipalities like those being developed or about to be developed elsewhere in the empire. They were trading bases, military posts for the defence of the empire and centres of Roman civilization and culture. 'Several became recognizable forerunners of the great cities of today'.

On leaving Spain Caesar spent some time in Gaul engaged in similar work. Then he set out for Rome, stopping at various places. With him for some of the time was his grand-nephew, Caius Octavius, grandson of his sister Julia, and his nephew Quintus Pedius, son of his other sister of the same name. He reached his country home at Lavicum, south of the capital, sometime early in September. There he rested, and during this time may have started his books on the civil war. There were three volumes, dealing with the Rubicon period, the settlement of Spain in 49, and the campaign in Greece ending with the death of Pompey and the first operations in Egypt. These books were of the same lucid and pure style as the Gallic War commentaries, and they were also notable for the generous appreciations he wrote of many of his enemies, especially Pompey.

He also made his will in which he left about three quarters of his huge fortune, several million pounds of it, to Octavius and the rest to Pedius, and to Lucius Pinarius, another great nephew. This was after leaving considerable amounts to favourite officers including Decimus Junius Brutus who had commanded the fleet that destroyed the Veneti in Gaul in 55 (page *117*) and who was to be a leading conspirator, and a cash donation to every citizen in Rome.

Octavius had made a great impression on Caesar while on his staff in Spain. This remarkably intelligent boy of seventeen, already noted for his hard and cold-blooded approach to life, seemed to grasp political problems with the same swiftness as his great uncle. It is possible that at this time Caesar was thinking of Octavius as a political as well as financial heir, and he made arrangements to adopt Octavius as his son.[1]

Caesar returned to Rome to triumph in October, an act which, since it celebrated the conquest of fellow Romans, gave great offence. In his absence in Spain a number of further honours had been decreed, which accelerated when the news of Munda was reported in Rome (at the end of April 45); a supplicatio of fifty days; Imperator as a hereditary title; permission to wear a laurel wreath all the time (which pleased him almost more than anything because of his baldness); a palace on the Quirinal hill to be built out of public funds; the consulship for ten years to be added to the dictatorship for ten years. More were to follow after the triumph. His birthday was declared a public holiday forever. The month of Quinctilis (in which he was born) was renamed Julius. Statues were to be set up all over Rome, and in the colonies where they had already begun to worship him as a god. His life was declared inviolable and the Senate was sworn to maintain it so. He was called Pater Patriae (Father of his Country). He was given a golden chair on which to sit in the Senate. And he was made

---

[1] Some historians after Caesar's time stated that he was the father of a son by Cleopatra, called Ptolemaeus, whom he allowed her to call Caesarion, and who was put to death by Augustus after Cleopatra's suicide in 30 BC. But this is almost certainly legendary. The boy was not mentioned in Caesar's will. It is not known when he was born. Suetonius records that Oppius actually wrote a pamphlet proving that the boy was nothing to do with his friend. Professor Grant speculates that, though Caesar had numerous affairs with women, only once did he father a child, Julia, and that was by his wife Cornelia. Possibly, therefore, the dictator became sterile.

dictator perpetuus, dictator for life.

How many of these extravagant honours he accepted we do not know. There are surviving coins bearing an inscription about his permanent dictatorship, which is very significant. Dictator perpetuus was unheard of; it seemed indistinguishable from rex, or king, a word that had been hated and feared by every Roman traditionally since the expulsion of Tarquin the Arrogant in 509 BC. Was this the reality of Caesar's power? Did he see that the only solution to Rome's overall problem, stability of government, lay in a monarchy, backed by a loyal and efficient civil service, able to call upon well-trained legions to deal with border confrontations, invasions and internal disturbances, with the power to guarantee continuity by choosing the right heir?

Caesar never expressed himself directly on this, though many of his words and actions led others to fear that this is what he aimed at. And this fear led them to oppose him, secretly because they could not do so openly. Before long, opposition grew into a conspiracy against his very life.

IX

PLOT AND MURDER

After Pharsalus, Caesar had been in much the same position as Sulla had in 82 BC. He could if he wanted have purged Rome of all his enemies, carried out his reforms and then laid down the dictatorship and retired to the country. Instead, he pardoned those of his enemies who had not escaped and tried to get them to work with him in rebuilding the state. This policy of reconciliation, which went hand-in-hand with his clemency in war, served only to build up resentment against his growing autocracy. By 44 he had greater power than was good for any man. Although he had done more for Rome and the empire than anyone before, he had chipped away at the old republican constitution so deeply that it was beyond restoration. Those who had tried to persuade him to carry out his reforms and then restore the old order, rule by the Senate and people, simply did not see that this was no longer relevant. There was an unbridgeable gap between him and those he sought to conciliate. It was emphasized by a number of things he said and did which, though individually trifling, when considered together gave him a reputation for arrogance which one would never have expected of him.

During the Munda triumph, one of the tribunes, Pontius Aquila, failed to stand up when Caesar's triumphal car passed the row of seats reserved for tribunes. Caesar was furious. He called out to him: "Hey! Aquila! You're a tribune, why don't you try to restore the Republic." This was a sarcastic reference to the powers of the tribunes, something he had long said he would restore on his way up to supreme power. But now he had made their powers about as ineffective as those of the consuls, praetors and quaestors. On another occasion, a delegation of the most important members of the Senate came to him to present some fresh honours while he was looking round his new buildings in the Forum. When they arrived he was sitting down discussing plans with the contractor, and he remained sitting. This gave great offence. He excused himself on the ground that he was not feeling well.[1] More than once he was heard to say that the republic was dead.

Caesar knew that the very nature of his work and his absolutism were making him unpopular. His life was so busy, so full and had so many demands made on it that from time to time he could not help giving offence. Once, when Cicero called upon him, he had to wait about for a long time. Caesar did not know his old friend – and political adversary – had been kept in the queue along with everyone else, and he said to Matius "I must be pretty unpopular if even old Cicero is kept waiting to see me. He of all people should be able to call whenever he wants."

He was aware that the opposition in the Senate was growing all the time, and doubtless he wondered whether there was any plot to depose him, or even kill him. He was heard to say more than once that it was more important for Rome than

---

[1] For much of his life Caesar suffered from a type of epilepsy which occasionally made him pass out without much warning. The attacks were usually mild. Perhaps he felt one coming on this occasion.

for himself that he should not die just yet. 'I have had all the power I want, but if anything were to happen to me, Rome will enjoy no peace. A far worse civil war will follow.' Perhaps he believed that the opposition would appreciate this and so be discouraged from forming a conspiracy. This could explain why in February he dismissed his Spanish bodyguard.

The atmosphere was becoming oppressive in Rome. Brilliant though he was at civil administration, eleven of the last 12 years of his life had been spent with his legions, devoted men who were extensions of his personality. Whatever the dangers, he had felt free, untroubled by niggling objections mixed with excessive flattery, which seemed to be all he could expect from the Senate. He longed to get back into battle dress, into his war saddle where he could order thousands of men in one or two clear cut directions for a well defined purpose, where his orders were law, and were obeyed without resistance.

The opportunity came in the East. Parthia, that powerful oriental kingdom squatting dangerously on the empire's eastern flank, had destroyed Crassus at Carrhae in 53 and the disaster remained unavenged. The ruler, Orodes I, was now aiding a Roman adventurer who claimed to be governor of Syria. If he could conquer Parthia, Caesar would make Rome mistress of the whole known world. He could equal the conquests of Alexander the Great, and do better than the great Macedonian because he had a ready-made imperial government structure with which to rule it. So he set in motion preparations for an enormous campaign; sixteen legions, 10,000 cavalry and archers, ships, stores, siege artillery, and all the other impedimenta of war. Embarkation date was fixed for 18th March 44.

Before that, the new order in Rome had to be left in capable hands. So he filled all the important magistracies for the next two years. Brutus and Cassius were to be among the sixteen new praetors (increased from ten), Antony was designated consul, with Caesar holding the other consulship until the 18th when his would pass to Dolabella. Aulus Hirtius and Caius Vibius Pansa, two generals who had served him well, were appointed consuls for 43, and Decimus Brutus and Lucius Munatius Plancus for 42.

Once the news of the Parthian campaign got out and the magisterial appointments were announced, the opposition in the Senate began to crystallize into a definite plot to remove Caesar from power. Bad as it was to be under a perpetual dictator in Rome, the thought of being governed from a distance through agents was too much. He had to be stopped from going to the East and death was the only way. The prime mover of the conspiracy was Caius Cassius. He enlisted the support of Decimus Brutus and Caius Trebonius. To attract more members he worked on Marcus Brutus who had a high reputation for integrity and who clung obstinately to the conception of the republic. Legend had it that he was a descendant of the Brutus who had driven Tarquin the Arrogant out of Rome in 509. Brutus yielded once he got it into his head that it was his duty to act on behalf of the republic. When Brutus agreed to be joint leader, several more senators joined. They kept their secret well.

Although some sixty senators (about six per cent of the total) are said to have been involved in the plot, we know the names of only about fifteen, including the ringleaders. They were all frightened men, for it is only when people become afraid that they get together to try to remove what is making them afraid. They dreaded the changes Caesar was making in the constitution under which they grew up. They knew not what the new order he was planning would do for them, their families, for Rome, despite the assurances he and his

Portrait bust of Mark Antony, Caesar's great friend. It shows something of his good looks and his jovial nature.

agents gave them. They were not able to comprehend a government run by one man permanently in charge, delegating much of his authority to men picked for their ability. This was their tragedy, and it was his, too.

Apart from being frightened, almost all the conspirators were also drawn together by the shallowest motives. Cassius had been pardoned, promoted, favoured, but resented it. Trebonius had let Caesar down several times but had been forgiven. Decimus Brutus may have been irked at having to wait two years for his consulship. L. Minucius Basilus, praetor in 45, had hoped for a provincial governorship but did not get it. He overlooked the huge cash sum given to him as a consolation. P. Servilius Casca was probably heavily in debt to Cassius. Brutus, on the other hand, had no grievances. But he had for some time been showered with flattery by many of the other conspirators, and this must have helped him justify to himself his role in the plot. Married to the daughter of Cato and the widow of Bibulus, both implacable enemies of Caesar in their time, Brutus will have been under heavy pressure to act against his benefactor – for that is what Caesar was. Brutus was a dreamer, and he may have honestly thought that the death of Caesar would lead to an easy restoration of the old order. If the monarch was removed, would not the idea of monarchy die? Thus he is said to have reasoned, and by so doing persuaded the other conspirators not to include Antony and Lepidus as victims of their attack.

The plot was carefully worked out. Caesar had first to be made much more unpopular before the populace who loved him would be persuaded to accept his assassination as necessary. So the conspirators picked on the theme of Caesar becoming King. They believed the people would not welcome his assumption of that title, no matter how much dictator perpetuus was the same thing.

Early in 44, a crown was found on the head of a statue of Caesar in the Forum. Two tribunes had it removed. When Caesar heard he accused them of having put it there. In February, he appeared at the festival of the Lupercalia, wearing the ceremonial costume of the ancient kings, one of the many honours he had received. He watched the festival from his golden chair. During the celebrations a crown was placed on his knees. At once he picked it up and gave it to the crowd saying, 'Take it to the Capitoline Temple. Jupiter Optimus Maximus is the only king of the Romans'.

Both these attempts to compromise Caesar were almost certainly contrived by the conspirators. There were others. Rumours were circulated of a prophecy that the Parthians could only be conquered by a king. People began to talk about Romulus, how he had been put to death for his absolutism.

You can suggest a lot by raking out historical similarities.

It seems that Caesar was warned that there was a plot in the wind. Hirtius and Pansa, and probably Balbus, too, urged him to recall his bodyguard, but he would not. 'If death must come,' he would say, 'let it come quickly.' Still he believed that no senator would risk the violence which would surely follow an assassination. As for the lunatic in the crowd, a hazard that any great man had to run, Caesar was sure he could take care of himself. His 'luck' would not desert him.

The Senate was due to meet on 15th March (the Ides of March in the Roman calendar), and Caesar had said he would attend. Possibly it was to receive the blessing of the senators for his Parthian campaign. The evening before he dined out at the home of his master of the horse, Lepidus. It had been a happy evening, though at one stage, as he was signing some letters, the conversation in the background drifted round to the subject of death. 'Let it come suddenly,' he interrupted. When he left for his house, it was raining.

Within about twelve hours he was dead, bleeding from twenty-three wounds, lying huddled round the base of a statue of Pompey, one of the many he had recently restored to their places of honour. The conspirators had been appallingly clumsy. Caesar's physician, Antistius, said afterwards that only one of the wounds had been fatal.

The senators ran out of the building, some holding aloft their daggers, crying out 'Liberty!' 'Freedom!', 'Long Live the Republic!' 'The tyrant is dead!' and so forth. Soon, the hall was empty, save for one or two of Caesar's personal servants who were in tears. Gently they lifted the lifeless body of the man who was to them a god, and carried it to his home, to the weeping Calpurnia, his widow, who was being comforted by Antony. During the previous night she had dreamt her Caesar was murdered and in the morning had

*Both sides of a coin struck to mark the murder of Caesar on the Ides of March,
44 BC. The portrait is of Brutus.*

begged him not to go down to the meeting. Death had come suddenly as he would have wished. And in death he was to be even more powerful than he had ever been in his life.

And when he was dead, men remembered his humanity and gentleness. Cicero applauded the deed but said Caesar never forgot anything except an injury. Caesar never failed a friend. He was incapable of petty hatred. When the poet Catullus had severely slandered him publicly, Caesar invited him to dinner. When Caesar and Oppius were travelling together through a wood, Oppius fell sick. Caesar insisted on Oppius using the only shelter available, a woodman's hut, while he slept outside on bare ground. When he embarked on his reconciliation policy he invited all his adversaries back to Rome. When Labienus deserted him for Pompey, Caesar sent all his personal luggage and property on to him. After the victory of Pharsalus, Pompey's correspondence and papers were brought to him. He ordered them to be burnt – unread. Even as he died, as Brutus plunged his sword into him, Caesar is said to have gasped: 'You, too, my son!' without the slightest shadow of reproach. 'Then burst his mighty heart', Shakespeare's Antony says.

The conspirators achieved precisely the opposite of what they hoped by their frightful deed. When they rushed from the hall into the streets screaming that they had brought freedom, they expected to be greeted with cheers and thanks. Instead they met sullenness, shock, sorrow, astonishment. The people had good cause to love him. When the conspirators pulled their daggers out of his body, they thought they had stemmed the tide of monarchy. Instead the monarchy they dreaded was established. When they broke their oath to protect him against harm, they believed they could alter the course of history and turn it backwards to the perpetuation of the republic. Instead, they found that Caesar had already changed it, irrevocably, and the Roman state was to develop exactly along the lines he planned. Among the things we know he conceived and began to put into practice were the filling of magisterial offices in advance, the extending of citizenship in the empire, the appointment of colonial people to seats in the Senate, and the encouragement of the growth of local government in the provinces.

The deed was not only a crime of the first magnitude, brutal, cowardly, treacherous and heart-rending to the thousands who loved him. It was also a blunder, the most senseless deed ever committed in history, the great German poet Goethe once said. The Roman world needed a strong master, and Caesar was just that. The republic became a monarchy backed by an army, and this new order gave Rome the stability it sought. We may not like this sort of order today, but 2000 years ago it proved to be an acceptable alternative to political and social chaos. In return for order men accorded the monarchs the reverence usually given to gods. The first of these man-gods was the dead Caesar, elevated to the heavens as Divus Julius, whose name Caesar was to be synonymous with the term emperor for the rest of Roman history.

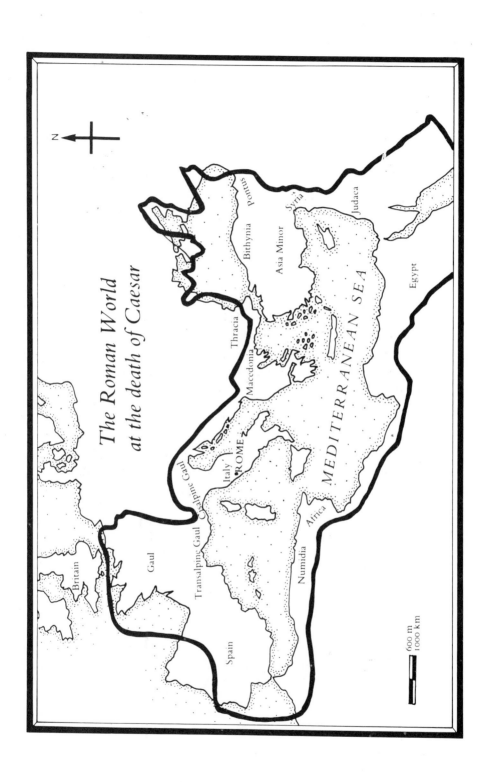

The Roman World
at the death of Caesar

N

Britain

Gaul

Transalpine Gaul

Cisalpine Gaul

Italy

ROME

Spain

Numidia

Africa

MEDITERRANEAN SEA

Thracia

Macedonia

Bithynia

Pontus

Asia Minor

Syria

Judaea

Egypt

600 m
1000 km

GLOSSARY

ACTA DIURNA   A daily register of public acts. It was introduced
by Caesar during his first consulship (59 BC), and it aimed to
keep the public informed of government and imperial
business.

AEDILE   The third grade of magistrate. Aediles were responsible
for looking after the city of Rome, its corn supplies, its
municipal regulations (including traffic, markets, water supplies, public buildings) and its Games.

CONSUL   The highest grade of magistrate. There were two
elected every year, and between them they were heads of the
government and they presided over the Senate. Ex-consuls
were called consulars and were eligible for the highest
provincial governorships or Roman army commands.

DICTATOR PERPETUUS   A dictator (or supreme head of the state)
was, until Sulla's time, only appointed in times of extreme
emergency, and his term was limited to six months. Sulla was
dictator for nearly four years. Caesar held the office for three
spells and then it became a permanent appointment. This was
the meaning of the title Dictator Perpetuus.

FORUM   The main square in a town, generally flanked by temples
and public buildings. In Rome, the Forum Romanum was
the principal centre of all kinds of activity. Caesar built his
own forum nearby. So did Augustus and Trajan.

IDES OF MARCH   Every Roman month had three principal days;
the Kalends, the Nones and the Ides. The Kalends were the
1st day, the Nones usually the 5th and the Ides usually the 13th.
But in March, May, July and October the Nones were the
7th and the Ides the 15th. These three days were the points
from which the other days were counted backwards. The
Romans included the days at both ends. For days before the
Kalends, the rule was to subtract the day of the month from
the number of days in the month increased by two. For days
before the Nones or Ides they subtracted from the day on which
they fell, increased by one. For example, May 30th was 'ante
diem tertium Kal. Jun.' (on the third day before the Kalends
of June). And March 11th was 'ante diem quintum Id. Mar.'

(on the fifth day before the Ides of March).

IMPERATOR   Originally, when a commander won a victory in war, his troops saluted him as Imperator. Caesar was declared Imperator in perpetuity, and Augustus and his successors assumed it as one of their titles. The English rendering is emperor.

LUPERCALIA   The festival of the Lupercalia was on 15th February, and was held to honour the luperci, or she-wolves. The founder of the city, Romulus, and his brother Remus, were believed to have been orphaned as babies and suckled by a she-wolf.

OPTIMATES   Broadly speaking, the Optimates were senators and their supporters who did not want changes in the existing order of republican government in Rome and the provinces. They resisted change even when it was obviously very necessary.

OVATIO   An ovatio was a reduced form of triumph (q.v.) in which the victorious commander wore a wreath of myrtle instead of laurel. Crassus was awarded an ovatio for his defeat of Spartacus (p. *72*).

POPULARES   These were those senators and members of the plebeian classes who wanted to alter the existing order of Roman government. They were often, though not always (such as in the case of Catilina), reformers who really did want to see the city and its empire governed better.

PRAETOR   The magistracy next in seniority to consul. Praetors were judges in the law courts. Their term of office was for a year. At the end they were eligible for appointment as governors of provinces.

PRIESTHOOD   Roman religion was a highly organized business which developed over the centuries. By Caesar's time there were three important colleges of priesthood, whose members were usually drawn from the Senatorial families. One of the colleges was the college (or order) of Pontiffs, which generally presided over the national religion. The head of this order was the Pontifex Maximus, an office Caesar won by election in 63. Priests in this order were called pontifices. Lower down the scale, young sons of prominent senators might be appointed as priests in one or other of the colleges. Caesar was nominated a priest of Jupiter when he was only 13. The Romans believed in many gods to whom they prayed or sacrificed for a variety of reasons. Jupiter Optimus Maximus (Jupiter, Best and Greatest) was the principal god. Others included Mars, god of war, Minerva, goddess of wisdom, Vulcan, god of fire and light, Diana, goddess of hunting, etc. They also worshipped domestic gods who were supposed to watch over various household activities, and these were called 'lares' and 'penates'. The god Janus, who had two faces, kept an eye on who came in and who went out. A small image of Janus was hung on every door. Vesta, the goddess of life, was another important deity. A fire was kept burning for her all day and night.

As Roman territory expanded, more gods were adopted into the state religion, some from the lands they had conquered, especially Greece. By the time of the war against Hannibal, there were so many gods that some Romans had become confused. When the news of the disaster of Cannae reached the city in 216, people asked 'What god do we pray to now to get us out of trouble?'

PUBLICANI   These were businessmen who obtained from the government the job of collecting taxes in the provinces, for which they were paid generous commission. Publicani became very rich.

QUAESTOR   The first grade of magistry. Once you had become a quaestor you had a seat in the Senate. Quaestors managed the finances either at Rome or in the provinces under the governors.

ROSTRA   A raised platform in the Forum from which magistrates addressed the people of Rome.

STYLUS   A metal pointed pen with which to write on wax tablets.

SUBURRA   A poor part of Rome, not far from the Forum, near the Esquiline Hill.

SUPPLICATIO   A public prayer or thanksgiving. It came to mean a period of days set apart for public thanksgiving and celebration following a notable victory in war.

TRIBUNE   There were two kinds of tribunes, the tribuni plebis (tribunes of the people) and the military tribunes. The former were by far the more important. They were officers elected by the people to preserve their interests against the aristocracy and the Senate, and they held wide powers of veto, that is, blocking of senatorial bills. They were elected annually. They were entitled to be elected to the higher magistracies afterwards.

Tribunes' powers were drastically cut by Sulla, but were restored during the period 70 to 50 BC.

Military tribunes were subordinate commanders or senior staff officers in the army. There were usually six to a legion.

TRIUMPH   A ceremonial procession in Rome organized by a victorious general. The train consisted of the commander, his legions, collections of prisoners taken, and wagons loaded with booty. The procession came in through a gate and went up to the Temple of Jupiter Optimus Maximus (Jupiter, Best and Greatest) near the Capitoline Hill.

PRINCIPAL DATES OF CAESAR'S LIFE

BC

100   Birth of Caesar, 13th July.

84   Marries Cornelia, daughter of L. Cornelius Cinna, consul.

80   Service with Minucius Thermus in Asia. Visits king Nicomedes IV of Bithynia. Wins Civic Crown at siege of Mytilene.

78   Service with P. Servilius Vatia Isauricus in Asia.

77   First major prosecution in law courts, against Cn. Cornelius Dolabella.

75   Caesar captured by pirates.

73   Caesar elected a pontifex.

69   Quaestor, serving in Further Spain. Death of Cornelia.

67   Marries Pompeia.

65   Caesar elected aedile.

63   Caesar wins election as Pontifex Maximus. Speaks against death penalty for Catilina's leading supporters.

62   Becomes praetor. Divorces Pompeia after scandal of Bona Dea festivities.

61   Caesar appointed to governorship of Further Spain. Conquers Lusitania.

60   Caesar forms the Committee of Three (Triumvirate). Stands for consulship and is elected.

59   Serves as consul. Marries Calpurnia, daughter of L. Calpurnius Piso. His daughter Julia marries Pompey.

58   Governor of Cisalpine and Transalpine Gaul, and Illyricum. Defeats Helvetii and also Germans under Ariovistus.

57   Campaign against the Nervii.

56   Sea victory against Veneti. Conference at Luca; Committee of Three renewed.

55   Caesar crosses the Rhine. First Invasion of Britain. Pompey and Crassus consuls. Caesar's command in Gaul renewed for further five years.

54   Second expedition to Britain. Destruction of Sabinus and Cotta in northern Gaul. Death of Julia.

53   Crassus defeated and put to death at Carrhae in Syria.

52 Clodius murdered in Rome. Pompey appointed sole consul. Rebellion of Vercingetorix in Gaul. Caesar calls off siege of Gergovia, but defeats Vercingetorix at Alesia.

51 Publication of Caesar's Commentaries on the war in Gaul. End of war.

50 Caesar requested to disband his army. Agrees to do so if Pompey will do likewise.

49 Caesar, having failed to come to terms with Optimates, crosses the Rubicon. Civil War begins. Italy occupied swiftly. Pompey takes Optimates over the Greece. Caesar defeats Pompeian army in Spain. Caesar elected dictator for the first time.

48 Caesar resigns dictatorship and crosses to Greece. Pompey defeated at Pharsalus and murdered in Egypt. Caesar occupies Alexandria.

47 Caesar defeats Egyptians and confirms Cleopatra as queen of Egypt. He defeats Pharnaces at Zela. Appointed dictator for second time. Reaches Rome and begins reforms.

46 Labienus and Metellus Scipio defeated at Thapsus in North Africa. Caesar declared dictator for ten year period. Opens his new forum. Introduces important measures of reconstruction of the state. Celebrates four-fold triumph.

45 Cn. Pompeius (the Younger) and Labienus defeated at Munda in Spain. Both killed. Caesar appointed dictator for life (dictator perpetuus); loaded with honours by Senate. Makes will.

44 Conspiracy formed. Caesar makes preparations to lead army against Parthia. Appoints magistrates for period of absence. Murdered on Ides of March (15th) in the hall adjoining the Theatre of Pompey. After his death, Caesar is elevated to status of a god, Divus Julius.

READING LIST

The principal sources on Caesar's life from ancient times are:

Caesar Caesar himself wrote seven books about his campaigns in Gaul. An eighth book about them was written by Aulus Hirtius, one of his generals.

   Caesar also wrote three books on the Civil War, dealing with events up to the death of Pompey.

Cicero Cicero was Caesar's exact contemporary. A large number of his letters (many both to and from Caesar), speeches and political essays survive.

Sallust Sallust was another contemporary of Caesar. *The War of Catiline* and parts of his *Histories* refer to events in Caesar's life.

Appian Appian wrote a *History of Rome* in twenty-four volumes during the second century AD.

Dio Cassius In the third century AD he wrote a *History of Rome* in nineteen volumes, covering the years 68 to 10 BC.

Lucan Lucan was the author of *Pharsalia*, a long poem about the Civil War written in the first century AD.

Velleius Paterculus His *Roman Histories* were written in the period c. 20 BC to c. 30 AD.

Plutarch Plutarch's *Lives* were short biographies of principal Romans, including Julius Caesar and some of his contemporaries.

Suetonius Suetonius's *Lives of the Caesars* included Julius Caesar and his imperial successors.

Some of the books and histories have been translated. These are listed in one of the following sections.

BIOGRAPHIES OF CAESAR

JULIUS CAESAR AND ROME J. P. V. D. Balsdon (Pelican Books 1971)
JULIUS CAESAR John Buchan (Daily Express Publications 1935)
JULIUS CAESAR W. Warde Fowler (G. P. Putnam 1892)
JULIUS CAESAR Major General J. F. C. Fuller (Eyre and Spottiswoode 1965)
JULIUS CAESAR Professor Michael Grant (Weidenfeld and Nicolson 1969)
CAESAR, POLITICIAN AND STATESMAN Matthias Gelzer, trans. P. Needham (Blackwell 1969)

TRANSLATIONS

THE CONQUEST OF GAUL (COMMENTARIES) Caesar, trans. S.A. Handford (Penguin Classics 1956)
WAR COMMENTARIES Caesar, trans. Rex Warner (Mentor Books 1960)
SELECTED POLITICAL SPEECHES Cicero, trans. M. Grant (Penguin Classics 1969)
SELECTED WORKS Cicero, trans. M. Grant (Penguin Classics 1960)
PHARSALIA Lucan, trans. Robert Graves (Penguin Classics 1956)
THE FALL OF THE ROMAN REPUBLIC (six 'Lives') Plutarch, trans. Rex Warner (Penguin Classics 1958)
CONSPIRACY OF CATILINE Sallust, trans. S. A. Handford (Penguin Classics 1963)
TWELVE CAESARS Suetonius, trans. Robert Graves (Penguin Classics 1957)

OTHER BOOKS ABOUT CAESAR

TWELVE CENTURIES OF ROME G. P. Baker (Bell 1936)
THE ROMANS R. H. Barrow (Pelican Books 1961)
DAILY LIFE IN ANCIENT ROME Jerome Carcopino (Peregrine Books 1962)
HISTORY OF ROME Professor M. Cary (Macmillan 1951)
CICERO AND THE ROMAN REPUBLIC F. R. Cowell (Pelican Books 1956)
HISTORY OF ROME Theodor Mommsen, trans. Dickson (London 1872)
ROME: THE FIRST THOUSAND YEARS I. Montanelli (Collins 1962)
HISTORY OF ROME Cyril Robinson (Methuen 1956)
THE ROMAN REVOLUTION Sir Ronald Syme (Oxford Paperbacks 1960)

GENERAL BOOKS

CAESAR AS MAN OF LETTERS Sir Frank Adcock (Cambridge University Press 1956)
THE ROMAN REPUBLIC AND THE FOUNDER OF THE ROMAN EMPIRE T. Rice Holmes (Oxford University Press 1923)
SEVEN ROMAN STATESMEN Sir C. W. C. Oman (Arnold 1902)
YOUNG CAESAR (semi-fictional) Rex Warner (Collins 1958)
IMPERIAL CAESAR (semi-fictional) Rex Warner (Collins 1960)

ACKNOWLEDGEMENTS

Acknowledgement is due to the following for permission to reproduce illustrations:

ANTIKENSAMMLUNGEN Munchen page 27
THE TRUSTEES OF THE BRITISH MUSEUM pages 23 and 105
COLCHESTER AND ESSEX MUSEUM page 158
GALLERIA NAZIONALE D'ARTE MODERNA Rome page 21
GLOUCESTER CITY MUSEUM page 111
GIRAUDON, PARIS pages 104, 109, 49, and 107
INSTITUTO STORICO DELL' ARMA DEL GENIO Rome page 77
ITALIAN STATE TOURIST OFFICE page 46
LIBRARIE LAROUSSE page 31
MANSELL COLLECTION pages 26, 28, 70, 86, 89, 130, 142, 160–161, and 172
RADIO TIMES HULTON PICTURE LIBRARY page 146
NIGEL SUNTER page 153
MUSEO VATICANI Rome page 56
H. ROGER VIOLLET Paris page 175